Music and Meaning in the Mass

AnnaMaria Cardinalli

MUSIC *and* MEANING *in the* MASS

SOPHIA INSTITUTE PRESS
Manchester, New Hampshire

Sophia Institute Press
Box 5284, Manchester, NH 03108
1-800-888-9344

www.SophiaInstitute.com

Sophia Institute Press® is a registered trademark of Sophia Institute.

Paperback ISBN 978-1-64413-281-4

eBook ISBN 978-1-64413-282-1

Library of Congress Control Number: 2020941084

First printing

Contents

With Special Gratitude

I'd like to offer my deepest thanks to Giovanna Cardinalli, the foundress of Familia Victricis. She's a mother so wonderful that I rejoice to be her daughter twice! I am enormously grateful for the guidance of the intellectually illustrious Dr. John Barger, who championed the idea of a guidebook on the musical language of the liturgy and edited the manuscript. I owe so much to the entire team at Sophia Institute Press, especially the fantastic and patient copy editor Nora Malone. I'm humbled by having astonishingly talented friends who reviewed portions of the text from artistic and musical perspectives respectively: Martha Goetz and Joseph Jones. Fr. Dennis Geng, OCD, Fr. Patrick Ekpada, OCD, and Fr. Remigius Ikpe, OCD, generously allowed me to rely upon the depths of their theological knowledge for support. I am indebted to those whose personal musical instruction has influenced me greatly: Janice Pantazelos and Craig Alden Dell. Finally, the true fatherly mentorship and direction of Fr. Dennis Geng, OCD, and the inspired preaching of my pastor, Fr. James Sanchez, have been indispensable to this work.

Music and Meaning in the Mass

Introduction

When I was just a little girl, so young that getting to watch TV past ten o'clock on a school night was a treat, my mom once let me stay up to hear Jay Leno's monologue. He told such an insightful joke, I never forgot it. "You may not realize this, but music is important," he said. "For instance, you should never confuse *Carmina Burana* with 'Karma Chameleon.'" Then, he demonstrated what he meant.

He cut to a battle montage from a movie. In slow motion, swordsmen clashed, horses reared, arrows rained down, and amidst the chaos, a hero bravely charged forward. The drama was set to "O Fortuna" from Carl Orff's *Carmina Burana*. In case the name doesn't draw the music to mind, it's what you've heard many times before overlaid on such a scene—a stirringly powerful lament with timpani drums thundering and sopranos wailing. It made the few seconds of the movie clip exciting and the hero's charge deeply moving.

"Now watch," said Jay. He replayed the exact same video. However, he replaced the music with Boy George's catchy and cheerful hit "Karma Chameleon." Not one bit of the footage had changed, but suddenly, the scene was undeniably and hilariously funny. The sword fighting became farcical, the horses looked as if they were trying to sing along, and the villagers seemed to be skipping through the raining arrows.

The grandeur that existed just moments before was gone. Then, the hero charged. Although on the screen he performed exactly the same magnificent action that previously inspired our awe, this time he looked absolutely foolish. No one could be moved by his charge with that music playing, though it had resonated as tragic and majestic just moments before. Only the music changed, but the music changed everything.

When we are presented with an example as striking as this, we can all recognize that music has the ability to alter our perceptions dramatically, yet far fewer of us can explain why this happens. If we cannot explain why, then we cannot make conscious choices with regard to music's impact. However, a great many of us are charged with doing just that, not in something as lighthearted as a movie but in something so critical that the eternal fate of the world quite literally rests upon it.

I write for you, the deeply generous and gloriously talented musicians who accompany Catholic Masses—from professional directors to youth choristers. I urge you to recognize the great dignity and the crucial nature of your call, and I seek here to offer you the tools to wield the power of your art at the service of the Eucharistic Heart of Jesus on the altar. The devotion to Him that you inspire or inhibit either consoles or wounds Him, and the salvation of the souls He loves hangs in the balance. To Him and to the Immaculate Heart of Mary, I dedicate this book. *Viva Cristo Rey!*

1

The Language of Music

Music and Meaning

A wonderful article by K. E. Colombini in *Crisis Magazine* titled "Keep Sacred Music Sacred" featured the insightful words of Archbishop Alexander Sample of the Archdiocese of Portland in his pastoral letter *"Sing to the LORD a New Song."*[1] The archbishop states:

> Despite the Church's norms, the idea persists among some that the lyrics alone determine whether a song is sacred or secular, while the music is exempt from any liturgical criteria and may be of any style. This erroneous idea is not supported by the Church's norms.

Here, the archbishop expresses a fascinating understanding that is easily overlooked. Drawn out, he seems to say that music, independent of any text attached to it, is capable of conveying meaning and that its meaning may or may not be appropriate for liturgical

---

[1]   K. E. Columbini, "Keep Sacred Music Sacred," *Crisis Magazine*, February 27, 2019, https://www.crisismagazine.com/2019/keep-sacred-music-sacred. See also Most Reverend Alexander K. Sample, Pastoral Letter on Sacred Music in Divine Worship *"Sing to the LORD a New Song"* (January 25, 2019).

usage. The archbishop, it seems, recognizes the reality of a language of music.

To me, this begs a discussion of this language. Without a basic understanding of its terms, we might be as hopeless at applying it as the poor teenagers who fell victim to the now-passé fad of tattooing themselves with Chinese symbols. Without having any real knowledge of Asian languages beyond what they were told at the local tattoo parlor, they were as likely to find themselves branded with ads for laundry detergent as anything else.

This precise problem echoes the sentiment of Pope Francis when he speaks about the banality that has crept into liturgical music. To participants at a conference on sacred music in March of 2017, the Holy Father stated:

> At times, a certain mediocrity, superficiality, and banality have prevailed to the detriment of the beauty and intensity of the liturgical celebrations ... [hindering the faithful from] perceiving the mystery of God and participating in it with all the senses, both physical and spiritual.

There was a time when adherence to liturgical norms meant that parish musicians did not necessarily have to speak or understand the language of music; they needed only to recite it. The correct application of the language was left to centuries of tradition. However, if we today find ourselves exercising greater freedom, then with that freedom comes the responsibility of learning and applying the language appropriately.

How then, does the language work? We know that across time and across cultures, music demonstrates a uniquely powerful influence over our bodies, our emotions, and our minds. In fact, it possesses mechanisms for influence over each of those components of our humanity. It does that through its own three components—rhythm, harmony, and melody.

The Language of Music

Rhythm

Rhythm is often the first component we understand. Our bodies are inherently rhythmic, and the soothing rhythm of a mother's heartbeat, heard in the womb, could be called the first music we ever know. Rhythm is the reason a lullaby is effective at rocking a baby to sleep, a march is effective at making us feel like stomping, and a waltz is effective at making us feel like swaying. Rhythm speaks directly to our bodies and impels how we use them.

No one would be surprised at the suggestion that a John Philip Sousa number would be a poor choice to create the mood for a romantic dinner, even if it were set with otherwise appropriate words. A march's rhythm sends a message perfectly suited for marching — and generally unsuited for most anything else. Similarly, every rhythm communicates to our bodies something specific.

Harmony

Addressing the next component of our natures, harmony can convey emotional meaning very powerfully. If we keep the rhythm and melody of a bit of music the same but alter the harmony, its emotional message is immediately impacted. When seated at a piano, I can make Old McDonald's farm seem a tragic and foreboding place by changing a normally major key to minor. By making the same change in reverse, I can also make a funeral dirge seem ironic or cheerful.

If it's difficult to imagine this without an audible example, go on the Internet and search for "minor key versions of major key songs" (or the inverse). You'll get a plethora of videos of people having fun with the interesting effect. You'll hear advertising jingles sound ominous and horror movie themes sound uplifting. The principle alteration in all of these videos is simply how the familiar tunes are harmonized.

Music and Meaning in the Mass

Melody

Finally, among the three components, melody appeals primarily to our intellects. Melody immediately implies pattern, and our pattern-seeking minds leap, almost unbidden, at the game of predicting what's next, of constructing reasonable possibilities, and of seeking resolution and completion. To understand this, consider the unease you feel over an incomplete melody. Try singing something to yourself and linger on the second-to-last note. The sensation is a bit like the discomfort you feel when faced with an incomplete sentence, an unfinished story, or that one book that doesn't line up with the others on a shelf.

There is a movie in which a neighbor of Beethoven is playing the piano and stops abruptly to answer a knock at the door. The joke is that Beethoven, before losing his hearing, is so disconcerted by the incomplete line that he storms over to his neighbor's, barges in, and furiously plays the last note. We all have a similar impulse. The impact of melody on our minds is so noted that researchers have coined the term "the Mozart effect" to describe the influence that exposure to complex, well-constructed melody has on the intellectual development of children and the performance of adults in tasks of math and reasoning.

So, with rhythm, harmony, and melody, music conveys meaning.[2] As Archbishop Sample implied, the musical meaning that comes about from these components is entirely separate from any

---

[2] For those who are academically inclined with regard to music, I readily admit that my above discussion is a gross yet useful oversimplification. Aaron Copland, for instance, is said to have identified melody, harmony, rhythm, and tonal color as the essential components of music. Other scholars sometimes come up with lists much longer than his four. I argue, however, that the three principal qualities I address above are those that are indispensable to meaning. Other qualities, such as tone color (or timbre),

text that might then be applied. Performers, composers, and the architects of different musical styles can order and emphasize these components to suit the meaning they wish to convey.

Mozart — with his simultaneously creative and predictable use of melody — can make me seek and appreciate thoughtful solutions. Puccini, with his masterful command of harmony, can make me weep helplessly at even the most implausible operatic story lines. The compelling rhythms of a good Irish folk band can make me feel like standing up and fighting for what's right, even if I'm all alone in the living room.

We all feel these things, though perhaps we don't take the time to sort out why. None of it, however, is accidental. It is music communicating meaning through its own powerfully influential language.

Interestingly, in the examples above, diverse as they are, melody has primacy over harmony, and harmony has primacy over rhythm. While the styles each emphasize one aspect or another of music's components of influence to achieve their purposes, the three remain what we might call "properly ordered." They are prioritized in the same way that Catholic teaching, like that of St. Thomas Aquinas, calls upon us to organize our own selves — that is, with reason ruling our passions and with our passions taking their rightful place in the healthy and whole human composite of body and soul.

Put another way, we could say that ideally, our thinking should rule our emotions, and our thinking and emotions together should rule our bodies. Music can help us do this when it is constructed in the same way — when melody (which influences our mind) predominates over harmony (which influences our feelings), and melody and harmony together predominate over rhythm (which

---

tempo, and dynamics, warrant discussion in later chapters for the complementary roles they play in creating musical meaning.

influences us physically). When organized differently, music can also make it harder for us to remain in this balance.

To better imagine what I mean here, consider styles in which music's order of influence is scrambled or even inverted.[3] For instance, the violence we hear in the most extreme rap styles isn't contained only in the lyrics. It is music that eschews the primacy of melody for an exaggerated emphasis on an unceasingly aggressive rhythm with a secondary underlayer of emotionally tense harmony. For another example, who can forget the "Lambada," the piece of music claiming to be the most hypersexualized that existed? That was a promotional exaggeration, but nevertheless, imagine how inappropriate sacred text would be set in these styles.

While these extremes are never the case in practical usage, something along similar lines does occur when the music at Mass

---

[3]   If you'd like to dig deeper into the experience of "ordering" musical components, here's an example. Consider the "We Will Rock You" chorus popular at sporting events. It's ideally suited for getting people revved up for a physical challenge because it emphasizes rhythm while not disordering itself by deprioritizing melody or harmony. Sing it to yourself while stomping out and clapping the rhythmic part. Doing so feels good, right? The rhythm is much more pronounced than it would be in, say, a song about the ethereal beauty of the stars. However, it doesn't overwhelm the catchy sing-song melody, which has the playfulness of a children's taunt, and its implicit major harmony, which keeps the emotional tone light. Now, try to disorder it. Take the melody away, and just speak it in rhythm while stomping and clapping. That's far more aggressive, isn't it? Speed up the rhythm and say it angrily. Imagine how hostile a crowd would suddenly sound doing this. If you happen to have an instrument around, choose some harsh or unsettling chords to play underneath. Now, instead of something that makes you want to win at basketball, you have something that makes you feel more like inciting a riot! Disordered music almost never has a positive effect on its listener, as its influences run contrary to our best physical, emotional, and intellectual equilibrium.

seems to regard style as simply a backdrop for sacred text without taking into account the message contained in the music itself. I frequently hear this happen under the auspices of liturgical enculturation—whether such sensitivity is meant to appeal to a particular ethnic enclave or to contemporize the liturgy for a particular age group. Enculturation is absolutely laudable, but enculturation often isn't what's happening.

Real enculturation of liturgical music should take into account the musical language of the culture in question and use the appropriate musical "terms" in that language for the physical, emotional, and intellectual experiences appropriate to the liturgy. These include the particular culture's musical terms for things such as awe and reverence, penitence and sorrow, transcendent joy and wonder. I argue that the ability to call on these terms is the criteria for the appropriateness of music to the context of the Mass.

I am familiar with a Mass setting that, although the final three chords aren't contained in the sheet music, is set to a rhythm that always compels the parish pianist to finish each sacred response with "cha-cha-cha." True, the pianist shouldn't do that, but the music shouldn't compel the pianist to do so in the first place, as he is only responding naturally to the bodily pull of the rhythm. What is happening is that such a setting, instead of embracing and using the fullness and richness of the musical language of a given cultural group, has seized upon the most stereotypical sound associated with that culture.

Now, from experience, I'd venture to say that the sound most stereotypically and superficially identified with any culture is embodied in the song most frequently requested at that community's favorite watering hole at 8:00 p.m. on Saturday night. The outcome of basing one's enculturation of liturgical music on this is as painfully oversimplified as saying, "Well, German Americans of a certain age group like polkas, so at their parishes, the Gloria should sound something like "Roll Out the Barrel." And the Sanctus? Well, make sure it echoes that established theme."

Interestingly, if the makers of a new-and-enculturated Mass setting were interested in learning the musical language of a certain group, perhaps they should at least stay around the watering hole until midnight, when nostalgic songs that express heartbreak, regret, and the tender hope for reconciliation begin to take their turn on the jukebox or with the band. At that point, they might begin to hear a hint of what the Kyrie should sound like. But I digress.

> My point is this: music is a language, and that language has terms for physical, emotional, and logical meaning. To misuse those terms is to contradict the meaning of the text. Whether it is intentional or not, such a conflict creates an experience in the listener akin to a lie.

It is the same as if I were to say yes with my words while shaking my head, winking an eye, and visibly crossing my fingers, thus using my body language to say no.[4] Which message would I send by doing this? Wouldn't the text of my yes be not only contradicted but perhaps even overridden by the stronger communication of no via a more visceral language? While such a mismatch of music and message might generally just make for unsuccessful or ironic art or advertising, in the context of the Mass the lie becomes dangerous on a scale of eternal consequence.

Why Meaning Matters in the Mass

This danger cannot be overstated. One might wonder why, in a time of grave and tragic crisis in the Catholic Church and in the

---

[4] The meaning of these gestures, of course, can vary by culture.

world, a point about liturgical music would be given such weight. To wonder this, however, is almost to forget what it is that happens at the Mass. Forgetting that is to forget Christ Himself, which is precisely the reason we find ourselves in a moral mess.

Let's take one step back and ask ourselves: Why is music a part of Mass in the first place? Is it because Mass is a long hour full of droning readings, talks, and empty rote actions that must be periodically livened up by a little entertainment? The obvious answer is a wildly emphatic NO!

The responses of the Mass, the parts that are sung in union with the angels themselves (Luke 2:14; Isaiah 6:3) as the veil of time is ripped away and we stand in awe of Christ's very literal gift of self, are not there for our distraction. The musical responses are the almost-incomprehensible opportunity for us to *participate* in the event of greatest cosmic significance that has ever occurred—Christ's sacrifice—as He Himself becomes truly and physically present on the altar. If we have forgotten this, we have forgotten what it means to be Catholic, and liturgical music that has lied to us may be in great part to blame.

It is unfathomable enough that our physical senses deceive us when we behold Jesus in the Eucharist. He looks, tastes, smells, and feels like bread and wine. At least our ears should affirm the sacred Truth.

In order to be truthful, our responses at Mass need to employ, rather than ignore, the profoundly influential language of music to sound like what they mean.

If they do not do this, it is better for us simply to speak the responses truthfully than to sing them with our fingers musically crossed behind our backs, so to speak. If we sing, "Lord, have mercy," it had better sound like we are imploring God for just that, not asking to be tossed peanuts at a baseball game. "Holy, holy, holy" had better imply to the listener that He who is drawing near is in fact truly, inconceivably so.

When asked to choose the music to which you will walk down the main aisle of your church for your wedding, would you exclaim, "Oh, wouldn't some indistinct and emotionally uninvolving elevator music be just perfect?" No! You would certainly choose music with meaning appropriate to the moment. When you are to walk down that same aisle to be even more intimately united with God Himself in the Eucharist, why on Earth would the importance of the music be less?

Consider the impact the musical choice would have on the onlooker. Consider someone who was questioning the Faith, or perhaps a non-Catholic observer. Consider a Catholic who, over many years, is exposed to contradiction in music to sacred texts and sacred realities. If such a person attended your wedding, at which elevator music was the selection for your procession, would they leave with the impression that something momentous had occurred?

The Parish Musician, a Heroic Herald

Is this a problem that is easily solved? I offer a hope-filled yes! Mass by Mass, it can be solved by *you*, the parish musician who gives of yourself to serve God and help save souls — if you have three very attainable things:

1. The first is a deep appreciation of the unparalleled importance and dignity of your work. This book will seek to enliven your Eucharistic devotion and assist you in becoming more vividly aware of the theological realities of the Mass, particularly with regard to the function of the musical responses. With it, I pray you come to know the fathomless wonder that you are welcoming Jesus Himself on the altar and leading souls to recognize

and love Him there. There can exist no greater artistic purpose than this.

2. To accomplish this purpose, you must be familiar with the principles of communicating musical meaning. Again, this book addresses them, and they are not at all difficult to learn or employ. They simply aren't widely known because they are not naturally addressed when our musical background focuses us on "how to" play an instrument or sing rather than on music's deeper language. You will quickly be ahead of the vast majority of musicians in your expertise in this area.

3. Like a trumpeter at the forefront of a charge, you must have the means to lead the congregation's sung participation in the act of meeting Christ on the altar. Here, you will explore which musical tools and techniques encourage (or discourage) the congregation's proper engagement in their role. This is also knowledge that very few musicians possess.

These three understandings will equip you for a heroic mission! First, they will ensure that the musical choices you make accord with the truth of the sacred texts you sing. Second, they will allow the faithful a full experience of their meaning.[5]

It should be clear from my suggestions above that I am not here advocating a particular musical style in the liturgy, though certain styles easily solve the problem of musical meaning matching sacred texts, which is the very reason they existed in the first place and why

---

[5] Because some of these musical tools are even better communicated with an instrument in hand, Sophia Institute Press, along with my arts-oriented Association of the Faithful, Familia Victricis, plans to offer supplements in online formats and through workshops wherever they are requested. The current website for these offerings is www.musicofthemass.org.

tradition upheld them. However, those styles can require specific training or familiarity, often acquired over a lifetime of exposure to the artistic heritage and culture of Catholicism. That is exposure you may not have as of today, and today is my concern.

I am thrilled by the existence of programs that seek to reeducate the Catholic faithful in these traditions and believe that in the long term they will have great success in renewing Eucharistic devotion. In fact, I believe them essential. However, my immediate concern is what happens on the altar right now — even before such a reintegration of tradition can have its vital effect — so I hope to offer here as expedient an emergency remedy as is possible.

What is at the root of my urgent concern?

Jesus Himself.

Today, Christ is present on the altar, just as He was present on the Cross at Calvary. On the altar as at Calvary, His heartbreak increases as His sacrifice is witnessed by indifferent crowds who do not recognize Him. We are those crowds, encouraged by music that whispers "That's not God. He's not here. Nothing important is taking place." Nevertheless, His Sacred Heart is as exposed to us in the Eucharist as it was when it was pierced by a lance or when He said to St. Margaret Mary:

> Behold the Heart that has so loved men that it has spared nothing ... and in return, I receive from the greater part only ingratitude, by their irreverence and sacrilege, and by the coldness and contempt they have for Me in this Sacrament.

Let us stir up our sentiments of warmth and reverence and love so that Christ today on the altar is received with comprehension and desire in our minds, our hearts, and our bodies. Nothing less than this is the importance of ensuring that truthful music accompanies the Mass. Your heroic mission as a musician, in the end, consoles the Heart of Jesus Himself.

2

The Miracle of the Mass

The Evidence of Human Witness

Not long before I wrote this, Notre Dame Cathedral in Paris was ravaged by fire. Watching the spire collapse sent a sickening shock that to many Americans was reminiscent of seeing the Twin Towers fall on 9/11. People of all walks of life, and of all beliefs or unbelief, sincerely mourn its loss because the cathedral was truly among the world's greatest treasures of art, architecture, history, and human effort. It was a global cultural loss on a scale that is hard to imagine or accept.

Far more terrible than all of this, however, was a graver danger in the blaze. At risk was something of immensely greater value than the cathedral, its history and meaning, and everything else in it combined. Father Jean-Marc Fournier knew it.

Father Fournier is an Afghan War veteran known for responding immediately to the scenes of some of the worst terrorist attacks that France has faced, administering the sacraments to the dying. A bespectacled middle-aged priest with an impressive mustache, he's also a chaplain of the Paris Fire Department. Being a chaplain doesn't typically necessitate running headlong into burning buildings in mid-collapse, but that's just what Father Fournier did when his position got him close enough to the Notre Dame fire.

Music and Meaning in the Mass

Surely, even among great treasures, no *thing* is worth the risk to life that the good Father took. However, a person is always worth such risk. Father Fournier ran in for a Person. He saved Jesus in the Blessed Sacrament from the fire.

After that, he also managed to preserve some precious relics, but those things weren't his first concern. Jesus was. Physically present in the Eucharist, God allowed Himself to be as vulnerable in that fire as He was when He became incarnate as an Infant — and as in need of our loving care, protection, and reverence. Father Fournier's actions protected Christ as truly and precisely as if he had snatched the Baby Jesus out of the arms of Herod's soldiers.

Father Fournier's actions aren't unique.[6] They are simply a recent link in a chain of Faith that goes back to the earliest Christians and continues today. Saint Tarcisius, just a young boy, died a martyr in first-century Rome solely to keep the Blessed Sacrament out of curious and violent hands. A little girl in modern Communist China who inspired the life of Venerable Fulton Sheen did the same.[7] These brave children, and many souls like them, clearly knew *Who*, not what, they were protecting.

In the face of that kind of heroism, we can begin to see how emphatically Catholicism teaches that Jesus Himself is literally

---

[6] While similar examples abound, the following moving article describes the martyrdom of an American priest and nun, unknown to the world but beloved to their local community, who died martyrs trying to save Jesus from a church fire in New York: Nicholas Wolfram Smith, "Ordinary Heroes, Martyrs for the Eucharist," *National Catholic Register*, March 3, 2017, http://www.ncregister.com/daily-news/ordinary-heroes-martyrs-for-the-eucharist.

[7] This is recounted in Bishop Fulton Sheen's book *St. Thérèse: A Treasured Love Story* (Irving, TX: Basilica Press, 2007), 30–36, but the story of the anonymous little heroine is a regular, almost legendary, fixture in much of Catholic culture, appearing whenever sacrifice for the sake of the Eucharist is discussed.

present in the Eucharist. It's only with this understanding that we can approach the majesty of the Mass or receive the grace that our Church and our world so desperately need. If we're parish musicians, it's only with an understanding like Father Fournier's that we can accompany the Mass appropriately.

The Remedy for Human Weakness

So, why do we believe it? And, if we don't believe it, why not? Have we forgotten? Have we never been told? Is something else failing to move or convince us?

A 2019 study by the Pew Research Group revealed the disturbing statistic that only one-third of Americans who call themselves Catholic believe in the Real Presence of Jesus in the Eucharist.[8] Those who are weekly Massgoers believe in greater numbers. It seems an obvious deduction that those who aren't going to Mass aren't doing so because they don't realize the truth of the miracle that's occurring there.

Once someone possesses that understanding, it's hard to imagine that anything could keep that person away. Certainly no persecuting army can keep Christians who know this truth from the celebration of the Mass. We sometimes remember the brave Christians of the first centuries who celebrated Mass in the catacombs of Rome and protected Jesus in the Eucharist, such as Saint Tarcisius, or maybe those intrepid Irish Catholics who managed to celebrate Mass in

---

[8]   See "Most Weekly Mass-Goers Believe in Transubstantiation; Most Other Catholics Do Not," Pew Research, August 5, 2019, https://www.pewresearch.org/fact-tank/2019/08/05/transubstantiation-eucharist-u-s-catholics/ft_19-08-05_transubstantiation_most-weekly-mass-goers-believe-transubstantiation-most-other-catholics-do-not/.

secret places when being caught was deadly, but we think of those times as somehow past.

Why? Recent Vatican research concludes that Christians today face the worst persecution in history.[9] Untold and underreported numbers of people risk death and are martyred throughout the Middle East, Africa, China, India, and elsewhere just for the chance to be present and receive Jesus at one Mass, and their priests die for offering those Masses.

On the subject of child martyrs for the Eucharist, the young brother and sister Sharon Stephen Santhakumar and Sarah Epzhibah Santhakumar were killed in Sri Lanka on Easter Day of 2019. I was movingly reminded of this by one of my little students preparing for her First Holy Communion, whose family recently immigrated to the United States from an area near the bombings that took the lives of the martyrs she so admires. Would that all of my students were able to experience the intense value that she sees in being able to receive her First Communion safely! Would that every family in the parish, like hers, understood that the Eucharist is worth either uprooting or losing one's life to receive!

Interestingly, when I ask if she has completed her assignments, her mom always replies, "Yes, and she has been learning and prac-ticing many hymns as well!" The family's emphasis on music as an expression of their Catholic Faith is incredibly strong, especially as a means of imparting preparedness for the Eucharist to their daughter. In fact, their emphasis on the importance of music in relation to their Faith is so great that, unlike my students born in the United States, she learns hymns at home whether I assign them or not.

---

[9] See "Christians Facing Worst Persecution in History, Report Says," *Catholic Herald*, October 12, 2017, https://catholicherald. co.uk/news/2017/10/12/christians-facing-worst-persecution-in-history-report-says/.

I see a similarly moving parallel in the experiences of my Spiritual Director, a brilliant and fiercely heroic Carmelite priest, who has spent countless years as a missionary in the heart of Kenya. He occasionally sends me videos of liturgies there. The music is irresistibly beautiful. While profoundly inculturated in musical terms specific to its local community, it compels participation and points unmistakably to the sacred. Not surprisingly, the Catholic population near him is suffering no lack of orthodoxy with regard to Christ's Real Presence in the Eucharist. Also not surprisingly, they do this amid the very real danger of persecution.[10]

In comparison, why are we American and other Western Catholics so lukewarm? The answer is complex, but if our approach to music has played any part in creating a misunderstanding of the Mass, so that there doesn't seem any reason to go, let alone anything to die for, can music also help us return to the certainty of the Real Presence of Jesus that leads to the kind of heroism we see elsewhere? I know this seems a simplistic solution, but my time in Iraq and Afghanistan taught me something fundamental about our human hearts when they are faced with the reality of war.

Few things solidify your courage as much as music, whether it's chanting along with your unit as you run together, playing a favorite rallying song as loud as you can before you leave your base on patrol, or being moved by your service's hymn or the National Anthem. From time immemorial, armies have been led by pipers, drummers, and banner bearers. They have often been the youngest and smallest of the troupe, but in a real way, theirs are the most

[10] Catholic News Service, "Service Draws Attention to Persecution, Killing of African Christians," *National Catholic Reporter*, July 2, 2015, https://www.ncronline.org/news/world/service-draws-attention-persecution-killing-african-christians.

powerful weapons. Their art makes clear the group's truth and purpose and gives it the daring to proceed.

I think of young Saint Joan of Arc leading armies with the banner of the Lamb, or little Saint José Sánchez del Rio bearing the Guadalupe banner in the Cristero War.[11] Will Catholic musicians and artists lead us, the Church Militant, into a vibrant faith again? Will you be the one to raise a rally cry?

Faced with heroic examples, here is what is especially difficult to understand about our weak and namby-pamby lukewarmness. If a Publishers Clearing House van pulled up to your house with a check for a million dollars, would you open your door? If you won a dinner date with your favorite celebrity, would you go? Most of us would. We'd celebrate! We'd be giddy!

What if you were offered something of more value and could meet someone of much greater importance? Would you accept? The bizarre fact is that most of us end up saying no.

If an angel suddenly appeared to you and told you that Jesus, the Lord God Himself, accompanied and adored by the whole host of Heaven, would be visiting your neighborhood Catholic church, and was doing so just so He could personally give you unfathomable gifts, including the gift of His entire Self, would you go down the block to see Him? What if a mad scientist told you that you could have a ride in a time machine and be present at the foot of the Cross to witness Jesus' sacrifice? Even more wildly, what if your presence there would mean the world to Jesus?

What if just seeing you there with His Mother and Saint John and Saint Mary Magdalen, when all His other friends had abandoned Him, and knowing you love Him enough to have come,

---

[11]   See Gretchen Filz, "St. Jose Sanchez del Rio: Child Soldier and Martyr of the Cristero War," *GetFed* (blog), October 20, 2016, https://www.getfed.com/st-jose-sanchez-del-rio-cristero-war-5910/.

would make His suffering more bearable?[12] What if Jesus longed for you to be with Him just then? Would you refuse to go?

Outlandish as these claims seem, they are the absolute truth. Yet, in the face of these extraordinary offers, we refuse. Do we not understand the truth? Have we forgotten?

If we are to be led into battle by our song, then musicians and artists must be the first to understand and live by this truth again. For those who might not hold the faith of Saint Tarcisius or Saint José Sánchez del Rio or good Father Fournier, the question is, why should we believe in the Real Presence of Jesus in the Eucharist? Why should we believe He is as present in His Body, Blood, Soul, and Divinity now on the altar as He was when He walked among us, and that He longs for us to meet Him there?

Is there both scriptural *and* scientific evidence? And might we be so unfathomably loved by God that He is that literally present with us today—with you and me as much as He was with His disciples or Martha and Mary Magdalen or anyone in the Bible we might

[12] Do you know why Saint John called himself "the beloved disciple" at such moments in Scripture (John 19:26)? He didn't do it to make himself sound special or because he didn't know how to spell "me." He did it because in the wisdom of God's Word, "the beloved disciple" can also mean you. You, Jesus' beloved disciple, can choose to be present at the foot of the Cross when the sacrifice of Calvary is made present at the Mass, as our perceptions of time and space are irrelevant to God's. Or, you can leave Jesus alone in His suffering, as did all the other disciples. The choice is always ours, but Jesus longs for us to choose Him. Interestingly, in the next passage, Jesus gives "His beloved disciple" Mary as his own Mother. God is never outdone in generosity. When we accompany Him to the foot of the Cross, Jesus gives us this most unbelievable gift—the Queen of the Universe as our own Mom. In the same way Jesus gave us a relationship with the God so intimate we could call Him "Abba," or "Daddy" (Matthew 6:9, Luke 11:2), we can likewise dare to call Mary our "Mamma." The mind can melt at these things!

envy because they got to walk beside Him? Do we participate in the pages of Scripture that our poor human minds can perceive only as past and future while they are all present to God?

Is it all wildly true and a greater adventure and more consequential than our tamed Christianity ever seemed? Yes! Absolutely! And our music must say so! If our artists aren't impassioned, who is going to be?

There are brilliant apologists who beautifully explain the Real Presence — the reality of Christ's complete physical existence under the appearances of bread and wine in the Blessed Sacrament. Read all of them. Visit the websites of Sophia Institute for Teachers, Ascension Presents, EWTN, Catholic Answers, and Credible Catholic. You will find physicists and biblical scholars and biologists and priests and astounding people of every sort to explain it from each professional perspective. I am not such an apologist, but I am an artist, and I can explain what makes me passionate about the Mass.

The Evidence of Scripture and History

As the story of our parish's newest family revealed, along with my mom, I happen to have the great privilege of preparing children for their First Holy Communion. Mom and I are those little Italian and Spanish ladies who are always bringing cookies to class and incessantly pinching cheeks. Your parish probably has a version of us too, and that version probably prepared you for your First Holy Communion. Take a moment to revisit that time. I will start by sharing the same things that I share with the children, as they are as impactful to me today as they were when I was their age.

First, God's Word is true. When He says something, that thing is. Our third graders love a game I teach them because they love to say "boom!" and also because I act everything out as I say it.

I ask, "When God said, 'Let there be light,' what happened?"

They all yell back together, "BOOM! There was light!"

"And when God said something like 'Let there be the stars and the seas and the salamanders and the sharks?'"[13]

"BOOM! There were the stars and the seas and the salamanders and the sharks!"

I ask, "Now, is Jesus God?"

Our kids say, "Yeeeeees," in the singsong way only a class can.

I ask, "So, when a man was crippled, and Jesus said, 'Get up and walk,' what happened?"

"BOOM! He got up and walked!"

"And when a storm roared and the water raged and Jesus' friends got scared in their boat, when Jesus told the storm and water, 'Quiet! Be still!,' what happened?"

"BOOM! They were quiet and still!"

"And when a little girl died, and Jesus came to her and said, 'Little girl, get up,' what happened?"

"BOOM! The little girl got up!"

"And on the night before He died, when Jesus took bread and said, 'This is my Body,' what happened?"

The first time we do this, no one yells boom right away. A few brave and thoughtful hands go up. "That was His Body?" they ask.

I am so deeply moved that I melt inside to hear them say it for the first time, but I say "Well, when God says something, it's true, right?"

"Right!"

"Whatever He says. Even if it seems impossible to us. Like a dead girl being okay."

"Right!"

---

[13] Please don't confuse the playful poetry of this game with a science lesson. The children know that the ways in which God's word is true are as unlimited as His power.

"Or even something not being what it looks like?"

"Right!"

"So, if He takes a piece of bread and says, 'This is my Body'?"

"BOOM! That's His Body!"

"And if He takes a chalice of wine and says, 'This is my Blood'?"

"BOOM! That's His Blood!"

"Wait, wait, wait," someone might say, often a parent in the back. "Not everything Jesus said was literal. He spoke in meta-phors and parables. A lot! He would say things like 'I am the vine and you are the branches.' That didn't turn everybody into hydrangeas!"

That parent would be right. Jesus spoke in metaphoric lan-guage so much, in fact, that when He did mean something liter-ally, He would have to be extraordinarily clear about meaning it. For instance, He'd have to do things such as preface it by saying something like "Really, really, I'm actually telling you."

Preferably, for clarity, He would do this a few times, and then repeat the literal thing He meant over and over so there could be no mistake. Then, ideally, He would refuse to allow it to be understood figuratively. If doing so came at both great risk and enormous cost, we could be certain there was no way He could mean it figuratively, and we'd have to believe His actual words. This is exactly what Jesus did with regard to the idea of eating His flesh and drinking His blood in the sixth chapter of John.

> "I am the bread of life. Your ancestors ate the manna in the desert, but they died; this is the bread that comes down from heaven so that one may eat it and not die. I am the living bread that came down from heaven; whoever eats this bread will live forever; and the bread that I will give is my flesh for the life of the world." The Jews quarreled among themselves, saying, "How can this man give us [His] flesh to eat?"

Jesus said to them, "Amen, amen, I say to you, unless you eat the flesh of the Son of Man and drink his blood, you do not have life within you. Whoever eats [τρώγω] my flesh and drinks my blood has eternal life, and I will raise him on the last day. For my flesh is true food, and my blood is true drink. Whoever eats my flesh and drinks my blood remains in me and I in him. Just as the living Father sent me and I have life because of the Father, so also the one who feeds on me will have life because of me. This is the bread that came down from heaven. Unlike your ancestors who ate and still died, whoever eats this bread will live forever." These things he said while teaching in the synagogue in Capernaum.

Then many of his disciples who were listening said, "This saying is hard; who can accept it?" Since Jesus knew that his disciples were murmuring about this, he said to them, "Does this shock you? What if you were to see the Son of Man ascending to where he was before? It is the spirit that gives life, while the flesh is of no avail. The words I have spoken to you are spirit and life. But there are some of you who do not believe."

Jesus knew from the beginning the ones who would not believe and the one who would betray him. And he said, "For this reason I have told you that no one can come to me unless it is granted him by my Father." As a result of this, many of his disciples returned to their former way of life and no longer accompanied him.

Jesus then said to the Twelve, "Do you also want to leave?" Simon Peter answered him, "Master, to whom shall we go? You have the words of eternal life. (6:48–68)

You will want to read the whole chapter, since seeing the Word and relating to it directly is so powerful, and also since I will paraphrase it here, and my style of doing so will leave much to be desired. Still, you know the story. It starts with Jesus performing a miracle with food. He feeds thousands of hungry people with five loaves of bread and two fishes, and He's left with more leftovers than the amount of food He started with.

Incidentally, that last detail about the leftovers debunks the notion that thousands of people simply shared a teeny bit of food because Jesus had taught them to be polite. What actually took place was a stunning and exciting miracle, just like the miracle of turning water into wine that began Jesus' ministry (John 2:1–11). Both were a foretaste of the even more astounding miracle He is preparing His followers for in the Mass! But I am getting ahead of things.

The people He fed with the loaves and fishes are thrilled and start following Him for the free food and entertaining spectacle. Astoundingly, He walks across the sea to get away from them and catch up with Peter's boat, but the next day, the crowd shows up on the opposite shore. At this point, Jesus has the attention of many thousands of people.

They know from their Jewish tradition that God sends signs, so they ask Him for one so that they may believe. They ask to see something like the miracle in which their ancestors were fed in the desert with manna, the bread from Heaven, and they clearly expect another display and free lunch, along the lines of a supernatural first-century *Iron Chef* episode. Jesus obliges, but not in the way they expect.

He says, "If you're interested in bread from Heaven and want to see a miracle, you've got it. It's Me! I'm the miracle. I'm the true bread come down from Heaven. Your ancestors ate manna and still died, but if you eat my flesh and drink my blood, you will have eternal life. The bread that I will give is my flesh for the life of the world." To express this, He uses the formulation "Amen,

Amen, I say to you ..." or "Really, really, I'm actually telling you ..." and repeats Himself on the point seven times.

The crowd collectively says, "Eeeeeeew." The translation says they murmured, but I'm sure it sounded more like "Eeeeeeew." They asked, "Who does He think He is? He's not from Heaven, He's from Nazareth; and the idea of eating a living person is horrifying. What does He mean 'my flesh is bread,' and 'unless you eat my flesh and drink my blood, you shall not have life within you.' That's bizarre, disgusting, and He won't let it go. It's making us uncomfortable!"

The crowds go from murmuring to quarreling, but Jesus only doubles down on His point. Instead of just "eat my flesh," He beefs up the literal language by using a more visceral word like "scarf" or "gnaw" (in Greek, τρώγω—meaning to mash up in the mouth and swallow). It's a word so earthy and physical (and kind of gross) that it makes a spiritualized or figurative interpretation difficult. Then He goes on to make it impossible by saying, "My flesh is true (real, actual, literal) food, and my blood is true (real, actual, literal) drink." He couldn't have been clearer.

Of course, all of this makes perfect sense once Jesus institutes the Eucharist and consequently the Mass (Luke 22:19–20; Matthew 26:26–28; Mark 14:22–24; 1 Corinthians 11:23–25). In those passages, as our kids understood, Jesus says of bread, "This is my body," and of wine, "This is my blood," and His power makes it so. Every word He says is indeed the truth, even when, like the crowds in the Gospel, we can't possibly see how.

Then we come to the final test of Jesus' literal intent. People leave, saying, "I can't deal with this. It's too bizarre." If Jesus meant this teaching in a way that wasn't bizarre, the way He meant any of His other metaphors (e.g., something along the lines of "I am like a vine and you are like branches, remain in me to live," as opposed to the shocking teaching that "Really, really, my flesh is actually food and my blood is actually drink, and unless you eat and drink of it you will not have eternal life"), He would have stopped them. He would have explained.

Instead, He was willing to lose crowds of many thousands of followers, with the salvation of their souls — each infinitely precious to Him — in the balance. At profound cost, He refused to change the literalness of His teaching. At that point, everyone leaves Him but His original Twelve Apostles. His mission is reduced to where it began when He first walked the seashore, and there is the very real possibility that those few followers who are left will also abandon His message over this one teaching.

Probably heartbroken but unable to compromise the truth, He turns to them and says, "Do you also want to leave?" Good Saint Peter, the Rock on whom Christ founded His Church, gave the answer that should also spring to our hearts as Catholics. In John 6:68, he says "Master, to whom shall we go? You have the words of eternal life."

Yes, it's a bizarre teaching. It's hard to understand, though I suppose it wouldn't be that hard if you had recently seen Jesus turn water into wine and multiply a child's picnic to feed thousands. At that point, where would you draw the line as to what you're willing to believe God could and would do? Saint Peter says that there is no line. At what point could we tell God that He's got it wrong?

"Wait, wait, wait," again says the skeptic in us. "That's all great if you actually *had* seen those miracles, but we haven't. You're trying to use the Bible to convince us that an outlandish miracle occurs at the Mass, but all you are doing is using your religious texts to prove your religious point. Of course, it will all agree! However, if something that momentous were really happening, there must be nonreligious, empirical, scientific proof, observable to any onlooker."

There is. There is so much, and I promise I'll get there. First, just two more quick points for anyone who does accept Scripture as God's truthful and reliable Word.

I'm stuck on John 6 because I love the Gospel of John, but does it make sense from elsewhere in Scripture that we are to take Jesus' words literally and understand Him to be physically present in the Eucharist, which we must eat to have His life within us? For answers, we can look back to the Old Testament and forward to the early Church.

One awesome thing that God gives us in Scripture is prefigurement. He makes a promise, gives an example, and fulfills that promise according to the example, so that we can see it was His doing. This pattern helps us to recognize His hand. Passover is one of those examples of how God saves His people.

Remember that all the events of Holy Week take place over Passover, so God intends to make the direct lines of parallel very clear. In the Old Testament, God's people were saved by the sacrifice of a Lamb. Jesus is the Lamb of God. In the New Testament, we are saved by His sacrifice.

But how does the Passover sacrifice work? Let's not forget that if the Israelites did not *eat*[14] the Passover lamb, the victim of the sacrifice, the Passover was incomplete. God could have arranged

---

[14] Eating is important! I say this not only because I'm Italian. In Scripture, how did humanity fall? Through a forbidden meal. How is it saved? Through Christ's sacrifice—a commanded meal! Consider what the Passover sacrifice would be without a meal. Why, then, would we ever see less importance in the meal that is essential to Christ's sacrifice? Why would we waste the gift of His Body and His Blood when He tells us that unless we eat and drink it, we cannot have eternal life (John 6:53–54)? Our Lord is speaking His essential message to us even at the most fundamental level of our humanity. We know we must eat to have life. He longs to give us His eternal life!

things however He wanted—maybe even in a more PETA-friendly way. So why would God have them actually eat the lamb if not to prepare us to actually eat the Lamb (John 1:29)?

With regard to the New Testament, we can be certain from Saint Paul, too, that he and the early Church believed the Eucharist to be the literal, physical, actual Body and Blood of Jesus.[15] Why? Because he was gravely worried about the situation of anyone consuming it "unworthily"—that is, without "discerning the body" or recognizing Who it is that they are consuming.

In 1 Corinthians 11, Saint Paul says:

> Therefore, whoever eats the bread or drinks the cup of the Lord unworthily will have to answer for the body and blood of the Lord.
>
> A person should examine himself, and so eat the bread and drink the cup.
>
> For anyone who eats and drinks without discerning the body, eats and drinks judgment on himself. (vv. 27–29)

This is a scary passage. Saint Paul is saying that we could have to "answer for" His Body and Blood—that is, we could incur the guilt of physically harming or murdering Him—if we were to receive Him sacrilegiously, without realizing or caring about what we are

---

[15] It may be helpful to research what the early Church Fathers believed with regard to Jesus' Real Presence in the Eucharist. They were the closest to Jesus and the Apostles in time and culture to help us understand His words, and they often learned from the Apostles themselves. Resources abound online to help you begin your own investigation. A place to start is "What the Early Church Believed: The Real Presence," Catholic Answers, https://www.catholic.com/tract/the-real-presence. I particularly like a concise video by Matt Fradd: "What Early Christians Believed about The Eucharist," YouTube video, 13:46, posted July 1, 2020, https://www.youtube.com/watch?v=JbqxxPtjtw0&t=5s.

doing. (Paul wouldn't worry about the harm of murder if he didn't understand the victim to be a living, physical, human person.) Saint Paul is saying that anyone who receives the Eucharist this way (who "fails to discern the body" or to understand the Eucharist for Who it really is) warrants that judgment on his or her soul.

This is what I'm horribly afraid goes on today when we go to Mass without understanding what is happening, and here is where musicians might begin to understand the eternal consequences and profound importance of their work. They can help create an experience of the Mass in which it's easy to remember Whom we are receiving, or it's easy to forget. With this awareness, musicians can assist in leading our souls to salvation. However, while fear can be a good and necessary motivator, it's never the best motivator.

The Evidence of Science and Modernity

The supreme motivator is Love, and it is Love that will lead us to create art that best expresses and inspires devotion to Jesus in the Blessed Sacrament. Interestingly, it's to engender this compassionate Love for Jesus in the Blessed Sacrament where modern experience and scientific evidence for His Real Presence takes precedence. Jesus manifests His Real Presence in Eucharistic Hosts consecrated in the Catholic Mass quite often, and when He does so, profound truths are revealed to us about His suffering.

There are innumerable incidences like the one I'll share here, and they've occurred throughout every period of Christian history. I've chosen to focus on a very modern one because it means that we have the most advanced scientific tools and methods at our disposal. I am also limiting the examples because this is meant to be a brief book about music's role in fostering Eucharistic devotion, and there are wonderful books already in print by true scientific experts on Eucharistic miracles.

Eucharistic miracles involve the Blessed Sacrament shedding the usual appearance of bread and wine and taking on the appearance of flesh and blood. Most often, they take place when a consecrated Host has been treated irreverently (which calls to mind Saint Paul's somewhat chilling warning about having to answer for blood) or when the Eucharistic faith of a person or group is wavering. They also come about to encourage and console Catholics in their Faith. Either way, they exist to remind us Who and what the Eucharist actually is.

There are hoaxes, of course, so every case or claim is investigated with great suspicion and great care. That's the kind of investigation Archbishop Bergoglio, the future Pope Francis, ultimately had to initiate when his phone rang in 1996 and a disconcerted local priest reported that a consecrated Host at his parish had suffered mistreatment. By then, such an investigation could produce very detailed results.

Apparently, the Blessed Sacrament was found on the floor after a Mass. This means that someone took Jesus at Communion without intending to consume Him reverently and exposed Him to whatever could befall Him while lying on the floor. To me, His being trampled underfoot recalls the beatings and degradation He suffered en route to His Crucifixion. I'm sure He met blows from the sole of more than one executioner's sandal, and in circumstances like this, we add to that the insult of our feet.[16]

The first reaction of the priest, and the one prescribed by the Church in such circumstances, was to attempt to soak the Blessed

---

[16] Imagine! Jesus calls John the Baptist the greatest man who ever lived (Matthew 11:11). John the Baptist says he's not worthy even to untie Jesus' shoe (Luke 3:16). Then Jesus humbles Himself to such vulnerability that we trample Him with ours? It's horrifying!

Sacrament in pure water, so that the consecrated Host might simply dissolve away. The priest left the Blessed Sacrament in a small bowl of water in the tabernacle. Instead of dissolving, days later, the Blessed Sacrament started to appear red and congealed.

Perhaps a red mold was growing? Perhaps a fungus? By the eleventh day in the tabernacle, there was no appearance of bread at all, but instead, a red, globular, congealed mass suspended in the clear water.

The mass stayed in the tabernacle until the right people could be found for the investigation to determine the nature of the material. Those involved had to be highly respected professionals, unaffiliated with the Church, and the investigation had to be conducted blindly so that the researchers had no knowledge of the source of the material they were examining.

The forensic findings were ultimately more astounding and revealing than anyone could have imagined. I will summarize, but absolutely everyone should investigate these findings on their own.[17] Not only was the mass human flesh, but it could be specifically identified as cardiac muscle. Call to mind those pious pictures of Jesus' Sacred Heart your grandma loves. The Eucharist is literally Jesus' Sacred Heart.[18]

---

[17] Just google "Eucharistic miracle of Buenos Aires." Or visit Reason to Believe, https://reasontobelieve.com.au/eucharistic-miracle/, where much of the original research is preserved and presented by its first reporters.

[18] Though I promised not to list the many extensive Eucharistic miracles of our time for brevity, for anyone who would like to *see* the Eucharist as cardiac tissue visibly beating in a striking video of another recent verified miracle, see Philip Kosloski, "This Eucharistic Host Was Filmed Bleeding and Pulsating Like a Heart on Fire," Aleteia, June 17, 2019, https://aleteia.org/2019/06/17/this-eucharistic-host-was-filmed-bleeding-and-pulsating-like-a-heart-on-fire/.

Music and Meaning in the Mass

But the Sacred Heart is always pierced and bleeding, right? Tragically, yes. The cardiac tissue was perfused with white blood cells. That is the state of a heart which is close to death, drastically traumatized, and suffering its final agony. The Eucharist is Jesus' Sacred Heart in agony.

The investigators were then met with a source of confusion. They were forensics experts. How were they looking at a slide of tissue taken from a *living* heart? Had a vivisection taken place? What kind of person had tortured a man so, and how was the flesh still living? The Eucharist is Jesus' living Sacred Heart in agony.

I lose my breath there, but then I can almost hear questions that the most extremely skeptical minds would put forward. They go something like this: "Okay, so it was a blob of living cardiac tissue in the midst of a traumatic death, but how can we be sure it was Jesus?"

Ever wonder what Jesus' blood type is? It's AB+.[19] Every Eucharistic miracle that has been investigated and verified (even very ancient ones where the blood is still fresh enough to test, as it remains living blood, just like the heart is living tissue) is AB+.

"Okay, so it was a blob of living cardiac tissue in the midst of a traumatic death with the same blood type as other miracles, but that still doesn't mean it's Jesus'." Well, the technology finally existed at the time of the investigation to submit a sample for DNA testing. The white blood cells necessary for the test were fresh and healthy, and samples were submitted to three highly reputable labs, but a complete DNA profile could not be obtained.

Why? The sample had only maternal DNA information. There was no genetic material from a human father.

---

[19] Nick Hallett, "How Eucharistic Miracles Show Christ's Blood Type," *Catholic Herald*, June 15, 2017, https://catholicherald.co.uk/how-eucharistic-miracles-show-christs-blood-type/.

No hoax, however sophisticated, could produce these results. If your astonishment isn't complete, these results can be replicated from tissue sampled from the Blessed Sacrament in other parts of the world. The 2008 Eucharistic miracle of Sokolka was also recent enough for current technologies applied to the living tissue to produce findings utterly congruous with those of the miracle in Buenos Aires.[20]

We are left to grapple with the reality that on the altar at Mass is Our Lord Jesus Himself in His physical Person. The Church teaches us that the Eucharist is His whole living Self—His Body, Blood, Soul, and Divinity. Through these miracles, however, He chooses to show us in a special way His agonizing love.

Doubting Thomas asked to see and touch not only Our Lord but, by putting his hand into His side, the very wound of His Heart (John 20:24–29). This is what Jesus, with the same generosity, allows our skeptical generation likewise to examine with even greater empirical certainty, if, like Thomas, we require such evidence to believe. If we doubt like Thomas, can we not also now respond like Thomas when we are given all the assurance that science allows?

Is there anyone among us now who will not fall on his or her knees upon seeing the Blessed Sacrament and, broken with wonder, speak the truth with Thomas? His declaration, "My Lord and my God!" (John 20:28), must be genuinely our own before the Eucharist—a truth with which our music resounds. Now, how can we not respond with even more humbled, tender amazement when we realize that, whereas Our Lord showed Thomas His resurrected

---

[20] Again, the reader is urged to research the evidence of these events on their own. An excellent resource on Sokolka with which to begin is the book *Eucharistic Miracles of the World* with a Forward by Cardinal Burke, and Fr. Mike Gorring summarizes the findings in a brief video here: https://youtu.be/HYC_Hn8lCG0

Heart in the upper room, He exposes to us His *suffering* Heart on Calvary?

If nothing else will shatter our indifference and move a heart to compassion and love, will not suffering? As a little child, I can be mad at my brother, but if I see him fall off his bicycle and skin his knee, will I not forget my peeve and run to dry his tears? A mother can be furious at a teenage son for sneaking away with the car, but the moment she finds out there has been an accident, isn't her whole heart consumed with hope for her boy's safety and the desire to run to and comfort him?

Now, what about someone who died for you? What if someone loved you so much and so recklessly that, seeing you in danger, he took a bullet or ran into traffic to save you. How would you treat that person if you were right there as he bled away?

Would you love him back? Would you long to comfort and console him and give him your thanks? Would you be indifferent? Would you be bored? If you were to sing to him, how would it sound? If you were to sing to others of his heroism, how would it sound?

How much more should our compassion and love be for the perfectly good and innocent Jesus, who suffers the weight of each of our sins out of His wildly passionate love for us! This is literally Who we see on the altar and the circumstance in which we see Him. Jesus has been trying to express His suffering to our hardened hearts in extraordinary ways in recent times, as it seems we have forgotten how to love Him in the Eucharist, or that we should even try.

This message is part of almost all of the recognized and approved apparitions of the last several hundred years. How far out of the natural order has God gone to express this? How have we heeded it?

Let's again meditate on the words that Jesus spoke to Saint Margaret Mary when He revealed to her His Sacred Heart, now knowing that He reveals it to us too, on the altar at every Mass:

Behold the Heart that has so loved men that it has spared nothing ... and in return, I receive from the greater part only ingratitude, by their irreverence and sacrilege, and by the coldness and contempt they have for Me in this Sacrament.

Are we now moved to love Him and make Him loved? If you are gifted as a musician, are you willing to put the full power of your art at this service? If you have said yes, know that there are few things that are as effective in fostering Eucharistic devotion and consoling Jesus' suffering Heart as what you have just pledged. In the next chapters, I will explain why and how.

3

Musical Mastery in the Mass

The Direction of Perception

There have been two fairly recent social and psychological experiments that I find fascinating. The first involved a violinist on a subway. Researchers from the *Washington Post* recruited one of the most famous violinists of our day, Joshua Bell, and filmed him while he played in a DC Metro stop, dressed in plain clothes, with his case open for tips.[21] The response? For the most part, stunning indifference.

No one listened. Without the usual props that said, "This is important and beautiful and worth your attention," no one responded as if it was. Surrounded with cues that said, "This is unimportant and mundane," people responded as if it were, regardless of the fact that it was actually Joshua Bell playing some of the most beautiful music that exists, *on a Stradivarius*. Reality didn't matter. Perception did.

We all have experiences like this. I remember when I was working my way through college as a Spanish guitarist. "I was young

[21]   Michele Norris, "A Concert Violinist on the Metro?," NPR, April 11, 2007, https://www.npr.org/2007/04/11/9521098/a-concert-violinist-on-the-metro.

and needed the money," as they say, so I accepted every possible job. On Friday evening I would play at a Flamenco bar, and on Saturday I would perform as a soloist with a symphony.

At one point on a Friday night, I ran through the concerto that I would play on stage the next day. On his way out, a kind, thoughtful patron who had enjoyed the music tipped me a dollar, which was crumpled in his hand. Unfortunately, he was compelled to use the hand holding the crumpled dollar to stifle a beer-induced burp just before he handed it to me.

My mom saw this and, once she managed to stop giggling, made a profound observation, as she usually does. The next day, I would be paid thousands of dollars to do the same thing. People would dress in tails, sip champagne, and believe the whole event to be important. However, I wouldn't play a single note differently. In others' eyes, the same action would be worth either thousands or a single dollar, based solely on external trappings and perception.

That's what leads me to the next experiment — one that is often repeated and continually causes a great deal of concern to safety experts.[22] In it, psychologists set up a waiting room and hire people to act like test subjects. However, in the room, only one person at a time is a real test subject. Then they ring a fire alarm.

If the hired actors jump up and run out of the room, as if the alarm is significant, the test subject jumps up and runs out of the room, thinking it is significant. If the hired actors keep reading their magazines and doing their work and don't react as though it were important, the test subject doesn't get up or react as if it were

---

[22] "Dangerous Conformity," YouTube video, 8:23, posted September 25, 2011, by HeroicImaginationTV, https://youtu.be/vjP22DpYYh8.

important. Apparently, we often take our clues powerfully from the behavior of others around us, no matter how important reacting to the thing at stake might be.

That doesn't seem too wise. How was the test subject to know there wasn't really a fire? Is there a way to free ourselves and others from this danger? Yes, and it takes a certain kind of self-forgetful heroism. Someone has to behave in a nonconforming way — a way that responds to the truth of the situation regardless of the perceptions around them. That proceeds to change those perceptions and help them match up with reality.

The Joshua Bell experiment had one bright point. After hundreds of people passed by without listening, one woman stopped. One brave woman recognized who and what she was hearing. When she did, and when others simply saw her bearing — her rapt look of "wow!" and the fact that she found it worthwhile to stand still in the rushing crowd — more people began to do the same thing.

Because of that one woman, others finally saw who was there. Plus, the good woman expressed her amazement and thanks to Joshua. The genuineness of her gratitude and love may well have consoled him for the hour he spent in the subway, ignored and freely giving his music away.

Of course, I'm talking about the Mass and the need to recognize the reality of Jesus' presence. That was easier to do at one time than it is today, because traditionally we surrounded Jesus' arrival with trappings and cues and human behaviors that said He is really there. For instance, when we all once knelt to receive Christ on the tongue from the consecrated hands of a priest, the Blessed Sacrament protected by an altar linen from the danger of falling or contact with our hands, it was easy to feel as though something very out of the ordinary was happening and that Jesus was very literally present. Everything physically reminded us of the fact.

When we instead get in line to receive Jesus in our hands, much as we do to take a number at the deli counter, it is easy to feel that something very mundane is happening. In such circumstances, it is tragically understandable to forget that the Blessed Sacrament is fundamentally different from worldly things we encounter. Very little physically reminds us of the fact.

Many such changes add to the feeling of mundaneness. However, these feelings have no bearing on what is actually happening. What is actually happening is that Jesus is just as present on the altar in an extremely tepid, unmoving Mass as He is in a beautiful, reverent one. Those tepid Masses may indeed be the ones in which His suffering is the greatest, because He is more unloved and unconsoled there than elsewhere. Nevertheless, there He is.

To see Him there, now more than ever, takes the kind of heroism of the person who, despite the evidence of the environment or the behavior around him or her is able to say, "Wow! That's Joshua Bell! Let's listen and enjoy!" "Wow! That's a fire, let's get out and save ourselves!" "WOW! That's the Lord Jesus Himself! Let us adore!"

My musical friends, that can be you! It can be you very effectively because you have the highly influential voice of music with which to proclaim this truth! How do you use it?

A Musician's Examination of Conscience

Truth, beauty, and goodness are God's transcendental qualities. In order to speak truthfully about God's goodness, our music must be beautiful. One thing (though not the only thing) necessary for our music to be beautiful is that it be our very best.

This has all sorts of interesting implications. One Mass I attended will forever be etched in my mind for its beauty. There were no stained-glass windows and no high altar. We all attended in filthy clothes, everything smelled disgusting, and the singing was genuinely some of the worst I have ever heard. It was, however, truly our very best, and only for that reason was it beautiful.

We were in a very far-forward position of the U.S. Marines' advance into southern Afghanistan. Our chapel was a plywood lean-to that covered the folding-table altar. Our priest was young and skinny and exhausted, which only made his bravery more evident. Oh, but how grateful we were to see Jesus arrive there with us. The loud, heartfelt, and terrible singing of eighteen-year-old boys who still weren't entirely sure of their voices and may have been slightly deaf from artillery fire proclaimed it so.

Most American parishes, however, are not so deprived that they resemble an austere combat outpost, so our very best there should not look the same. If the situation at our own parishes is not so dire, and yet our music resembles that of the Marines in failing to meet certain very attainable standards which this section will explore, even if it is offered with as great a degree of devotion and enthusiasm as the Marines managed, it cannot be called beautiful. Without beauty, we are not speaking the truth about God in the Mass.

If, to any degree, this can be said of our music, why aren't we doing our best, and what can our best look like? I propose a miniature examination of conscience for musicians. It contains the questions I continually ask myself in my professional life and discuss with friends.

1. Why am I singing or playing an instrument?

The most frequent and beautiful response most of us will give is "I am doing it for God." If you are doing it for God, then, when you are alone in your room or waiting on your laundry, do you sing or play for Him? Do you make music in the world at large — at work or school or home or professionally — specifically for His glory? If not, why do you do so only at Mass?

2. If I am singing or playing only at Mass, why?

Are there other reasons for your making music at Mass? If there are, they aren't necessarily bad. They could include things such as enjoying the chance to socialize with your friends in the choir or desiring to display your God-given musical talent. Fortunately, there are many opportunities for these kinds of expressions outside the Mass.

To seek to do these other good things at Mass, when something profoundly critical is happening, is like saying you enjoy chatting with or entertaining doctors in the midst of open-heart surgery. In the Mass, our focus should be only on what's happening and on assisting. It's not a time for socializing or performance, because it's not about us; it's about Jesus.

Perhaps, instead, your real motivation for singing in the choir is that you desire to pray through song in community with others. That is extraordinarily beautiful! After all, Our Lord Himself says where two or three are gathered, He is present (Matthew 18:20), and Saint Augustine says that one who sings well prays twice, so praying in this way is powerful indeed.

However, participating in the choir that assists the sacrifice of the Mass isn't the way to pursue this goal as your principal aim. To fulfill this need, I recommend that those who desire only to pray in this way without the limits proper to the Mass take it upon themselves to organize devotional musical programs such as Taize services, praise and worship song nights, etc. This is another amazing way to serve your community through music.

3. Am I doing my best?

Many times, I hear people say, "I sing at Church because God loves me and He doesn't judge." We all know people who say this and then sing or play quite badly. Yes, it's true that God loves them and probably regards their off-key moments, if they are privately directed in praise to Him alone, with the warm pride of a parent watching a peewee soccer game. ("My kid almost hit that note!" He might exclaim to exasperated angels.)

However, at Mass, it is not only God who hears. The music at Mass influences the devotion and disposition of the human souls around us toward God, and this, in turn, either consoles or wounds Him on the altar. Though this implies a profound responsibility for the musician, it doesn't mean that every musician at Mass must be held to impossible standards.

It does mean that we should each consider seriously if we are making music with a sincere desire to bring souls to God, specifically to Christ in the Eucharist. If we are, then that intention alone will compel us, by conscience, to strive to improve. We will be motivated to practice and study, for instance.

Improvement, therefore, is the litmus test of our sincerity. If we are not improving, then we are not giving God our very best. This will remain true our entire lives as liturgical musicians, whatever our level of training or talent or achievement may be.

Yes, God loves us. The question here is our love for Him. Things such as a blasé acceptance of whatever level we are at as "good enough" for the Mass and an unwillingness to work to improve may be wounding Him. If we are doing this unwittingly, now's the time to adjust our course!

So, what kind of work do we need to do in order for our music to speak truthfully about Jesus in the Mass? Three kinds, and they're all accomplishable for every parish musician. We need to prioritize and pursue technical proficiency (the right notes must happen at the right time, played or sung correctly), expressiveness (the music must be more than correct notes in time), and appropriateness to the liturgy (which is where the language of music is taken into full account).

Music and Meaning in the Mass

Technical Proficiency (The Good)

Technical proficiency is straightforward. We can seek to improve it on our own, with help from instruction online, and with help from friends and teachers. The need for continual growth here never stops, whatever our level may be.

Does this call for a commitment of time and sometimes resources? Absolutely. If we have decided to respond to the call of serving as a liturgical musician, that means we desire to give a gift to God. We can give Him the gift He longs for most, which is to be known and loved in the Mass.

If that gift is limited to just a bit more than the time we would have spent at Mass anyway, and we never expend ourselves to make the gift better, how much of a gift is it? Most parents have received a quickly scratched "Happy Birthday" card on a scrap of paper, and they have received a heartfelt card a child spent a day trying to make. They know the difference. God does too.

I invite you now to take a moment to decide what you are willing to offer Him for the purpose of preparing this gift. In addition to going to weekly rehearsal, can you forgo a half-hour television show once or twice a week to practice for Him on your own? Can you get up fifteen minutes earlier or go to bed fifteen minutes later some days? As an unsought bonus, such little sacrifices often pay dividends in the spiritual life!

With regard to technical proficiency, we must, at the very least, be able to sing or play the right notes of the music we perform at Mass at the correct time (neither sharp nor flat, early nor late), and we should then seek to accomplish this with beautiful tone. It's uncertain to me if saying so sounds either obvious or harsh, but if no one is saying it, and no one is doing it, this is contributing enormously to the perception of unimportance in the Mass. I say this not for the sake of criticism but because when the Mass is perceived as unimportant, Jesus is more and more abandoned on the altar.

Would you be willing to do something that I myself admit to finding very scary, if you are doing it for Jesus' sake? Have you ever heard your own voice, perhaps on a phone message, and been shocked by its sound? For simple reasons of physiology and acoustics, our voices sound very different when heard resonating inside our own heads from the way they sound externally. Therefore, if we want to know if our singing is pleasing to anyone but ourselves, we have to record it.[23]

In our day of fancy phone features, you probably have in your pocket the ability to do this. If you record yourself and listen back, you will find faults. I've worked professionally as a musician for many years and promise you that I record myself and find faults every time I practice, and I have shed not a few tears over them.

In my case or yours, however, there is no need for those tears. Please let me share with you a great secret. It is not freedom from these faults that differentiates good musicians from poor ones — *it is the willingness to seek out and address them*. The mere willingness itself! In this way, progress in the musical life is not at all unlike progress in the spiritual life.

Rather than be reduced by faults, be improved by them! When you find an issue, do not let it discourage you, but work to fix it. No one who is unaware of a fault can improve, nor is anyone free of faults. Do not allow any feeling of dispiritedness to trick you into giving up on your work, as doing so would also contribute to Jesus' abandonment on the altar!

I promise that this very day, someone in a dressing room at the Metropolitan Opera or the Grand Ole Opry or whatever your favorite musical venue might be is recording a practice attempt on a phone, then calling a coach or teacher and saying, "Oh my

---

[23] Even though the physiological reasons don't equally apply, the same advice is good for instrumentalists as well.

goodness! I need to fix this." That inclination is the very reason why they are there. Now, bear in mind all the reasons that your work during the Mass is far more important than theirs at the concert hall.

It is with good reason that I mention a teacher with regard to singing. Despite being the most instinctive to use, the human voice is the most difficult instrument with which to gain proficiency because of two critical issues. Besides being impossible to hear accurately in real time for the acoustic reasons discussed,[24] it is also impossible in real time for a singer to see the muscles involved at work. We are both deaf and blind to our activity when singing.

Pianists or guitarists have the feedback of being able to watch their fingers on the keyboard or the fretboard for accuracy, while a singer has no such "check." This means that the only way to increase in mastery is with at least some professional voice training, to whatever degree this might be possible. Singers must learn to feel the correct positions of muscles they cannot watch, through live interaction with another person who understands the hidden function of those muscles.

If you adopt the same professional attitude as your favorite artists who check themselves against recordings and the input of others — if you even get excited at the idea of finding something to improve upon — you will never get "stuck" in your musical progress the way people often do. We must admit that we hear some church choirs persist in the same problems for many years. I suspect this is because if someone remains unaware of a fault, even if that person practices, he or she is just practicing to make that fault more and more deeply ingrained as a habit.

---

[24] Luciano Pavarotti is purported to have said, "It is a shame I cannot hear myself while I sing. Imagine how good I would be if I could!"

Here's the uplifting side of this realization. It means the key to making music well isn't some mysterious degree of talent or aptitude (although someone completely disinclined does not belong in a choir). Instead, the key is simply a highly attainable attitude of humility combined with a reasonable, genuine investment of effort.

None of our current liturgical music makes demands that an amateur musician cannot readily conquer with this approach, so no one should be offering music at Mass until he or she is at least able to execute it correctly. This might mean taking time at home to learn, some degree of investment in study, and embracing a practice of regular musical self-examination. God will cherish such a sacrificial and painstaking gift!

Expressiveness (*The Beautiful*)

Essential as it is, executing all of the necessary notes faultlessly should not be seen as an end. If it becomes our goal, it is akin to making the goal of language merely to say each word and believing if that is done, the message is communicated. No. One. Communicates. A. Message. While. Speaking. Like. This. The words or notes are simply the building blocks of the sentence or the line.

This is not easily discussed in written text, but it's worth trying an exercise anyway. Let's take the first line of a favorite hymn and sing it solely to accomplish the execution of each note. Be. Thou. My. Vision. O. Lord. Of. My. Heart. (Record this exercise on your phone if you're willing to try.)

Now, let's sing it in a line as if we mean "Be Thou my vision, O Lord of my heart!" When we sing with meaning, we give each note its proper place. Though we should not change the correct values or pitches of the notes, they are not, for instance, all sung with the same volume or emphasis.[25] (Extra points if you sing this

---

[25] Or, in musical terms, dynamics and phrasing.

one more time, but this time as if you're the young sightless monk who wrote the prayer, pleading with his entire heart. That's more like the expressiveness appropriate to Mass!)

Despite the example from a hymn, we also must remember that an expressive line is just as necessary from an instrument as it is from the voice. Imagine an instrumentalist who plays every note the same way, with exactly the same degree of emphasis. Is he or she effectively communicating?

Appropriateness (The True)

Now, with technique and expression in place, it is time to tackle the real questions about liturgical music and its usage. These decisions, made by musicians on the ground, parish by parish and Mass by Mass, can, as of this very day, help rebuild our recognition of our Lord on the altar and the transcendent reality of the Mass as our presence and participation at Calvary.

First, it must be restated that none of the responses in the Mass are interjections of entertainment. They each have a critical function whereby our prayers participate in the unfolding miracle. If these prayers are set to music, that music must accord with and intensify that purpose, not contradict it. In chapter 6, the role of each Mass response will be examined. However, as an exercise, and because of their contrast, let's briefly consider the Kyrie and the Sanctus now.

What is the purpose of the Kyrie? Jesus cannot enter and be welcomed into a sin-stained heart. If we have serious sin on our souls, we must seek the sacrament of Confession before receiving the Eucharist. However, venial sin and imperfections often accumulate on our souls like dust between one reception of the Eucharist and the next, and a dusty, dirty home is no welcoming place for our Lord.

The fact that we realize this points to the reality that the Blessed Sacrament is truly Our Lord Himself. To disregard it or minimize its importance would be to help to confuse the fact. So, to begin Mass, we consider our sins and pray for God's mercy, which renders souls already in the state of grace prepared to receive. The Kyrie pleads for that mercy, addressing the Risen Lord.

With that in mind, we should consider the three building blocks of musical meaning, starting with rhythm. If you have the choice between two settings of the Kyrie, which of them presents a rhythm closest to the sentiment of the prayer? Is it one that should impel us to move or to be still? Is it one that is bouncy and jovial, or is it one that is more even and somber? What tempo would be appropriate?

Next consider key and harmonization. This defines the mood of the prayer. Should the mood be sorrowful? Hopeful? Peaceful? Here we can exclude any settings where the mood is inappropriate—for instance, where it is flat or flippant or obliviously cheerful.

Finally, we consider melody. Among our options, is there a melody that best expresses pleading? One that rises and falls much as speech does to implore? That's our best choice. If not, we must exclude ones that contradict the prayer, such as those that may be overly ornate performance pieces that obscure the meaning of the words or those that are so simplistic as to fail to engage the listener.

These choices almost make themselves once the meaning of the prayer is compared with its musical components. Take the Sanctus for our next example. Why is the Sanctus part of the Mass, and what does our singing it accomplish? Again, it's there for a profound purpose, and it's not a distraction or a decoration. Instead, in the Sanctus, the veils that create our perceptions of distance in time and space are ripped to shreds.

Holy. Holy. Holy. To call God thrice holy is to participate in the worship of the angels (Isaiah 6:3; Revelation 4:8). They adore Christ's sacrifice in the Mass because they adore it on Calvary, and in the Sanctus, we *sing with them* in the incredible dignity of that act of worship. Similarly, to sing, "Blessed is He Who comes in the

Name of the Lord" is to participate in the worship of the crowds who cheered Jesus as He entered Jerusalem just prior to His Passion (Matthew 21:9, from Psalm 118:26).

Those are not empty words from the crowd. It was the greeting they yelled to recognize a long-awaited King of the line of David—one who they believed would restore the Kingdom. They were right. That is exactly what is happening in the Mass, and we, in the Sanctus, are able to cry out with them at the precise moment of their acknowledgment of Christ as King, consoling Him just before His Passion.

With what music must we do this? With what reverence? With what fervor? How would we exclaim it if we were there in Jerusalem to throw down our cloaks and our palms before Him on His donkey? The hidden reality is, to Him, we *are* there. He hears our prayer, our exultation, then and now. He is comforted by it, or wounded by our indifference in it, then and now. (Of course, there is no "then" and "now" in God's eyes, only in ours—but in the Mass, we begin to perceive and participate in this truth.)

Do we really want to be half-heartedly humming our hosannas on the Jerusalem street as He passes? Can we instead sing them in a way that makes known our love? Doing so will console Him and help others in the pews to do the same. Can we not lead this charge of praise?

It is with these realities in mind that we must then select (or compose, if God has given us such gifts) the setting of the Sanctus. Should the rhythm be stirring? Reverent? Should the key and harmonies be uplifting? Exultant? As we are singing to welcome a King, should the melody suggest majesty? Finally, shouldn't we reject musical choices that are diametrically opposed to these qualities?

These choices, and their impact, are in your hands, my brother and sister musicians. I thank God that in your faithfulness and love, you desire to dedicate the work and make the choices that will enkindle a recognition of the realities of the Mass. In the end, may they ultimately reignite our tepid devotion to Jesus as He is present on the altar. There is nothing, truly nothing, in this world that could be of greater significance.

4

Musical Leadership in the Mass

This chapter continues exploring technical tools for making meaningful music at Mass. Again, the silent written word here is a difficult medium for communicating information about sound. Therefore, multimedia supplements and live workshop events will follow at the website www.musicofthemass.org.

Even without these, however, I believe it is still possible to convey some of the most important points here on the page if readers are willing to engage their aural imaginations as examples are described. This can work only with your active cooperation. So, if I use an analogy or even a silly onomatopoeia to describe a sound, please take a moment to imagine it with me, and please know you have my genuine thanks for your extra engagement.

The Impact of Instrumentation

Does instrumentation matter? In what way? If a set of bagpipes and a banjo can both correctly execute all the notes required to accompany a song, then what difference does it make if the song is played on either?

Is that difference cultural or generational—something we might categorize as one of fashion? Perhaps we think so. For instance, we associate organs with the liturgical music of a previous generation and, wanting to identify as more fresh and accessible, decide pianos and guitars are more our style.

Being fresh and accessible are not goals to be disparaged, and no less laudable is the goal of preserving tradition. (I'm reminded of Saint Augustine's exclamation "O Beauty ever ancient, ever new!") However, I'd like to argue that the choice of instrumentation in liturgical music should have nothing to do with either of those goals.

Instead, I'd like to offer a new basis for the instrumental choices you make at your parish. I'd like to propose that the reason instrumentation matters has much more to do with the functional features of each instrument than any issue of taste. Ultimately, familiarity with the attributes of the tools you have at your disposal will help you make the best choices possible for the critical task at hand.

Beyond our first discussion of the essential musical elements of rhythm, harmony, and melody, the next musical attribute that can help us have a swiftly effective impact on the congregation's experience of music at Mass is *timbre*. Timbre is the "-ness" of any instrument's sound. It's the thing that allows your mind to recognize, "Aha! That's an accordion!" (and then beg for it to stop) when you hear one on a recording and can't see what's being played.[26]

Perhaps the component of timbre most relevant to our discussion is what I will term "sustain."[27] Different instruments have it

---

[26] It has been said that the definition of a gentleman is one who knows how to play the accordion and refrains.

[27] The Acoustical Society of America (ASA) Acoustical Terminology definition 12.09 of "timbre" is "that attribute of auditory sensation which enables a listener to judge that two nonidentical sounds, similarly presented and having the same loudness

to different degrees. What I mean is the ability of an instrument to hold a note for the duration of its value at a relatively unchanging volume (as opposed to a rapid tendency of the note to fade away).

For example, no matter the technique of the player, essentially, a piano can only go "plink." There is a rapid decay of sound after the initiation of each note. In contrast, a trumpet can go "tooooooooooot." Its note can be sustained at a more consistent volume until the trumpeter runs out of breath.

However, unlike the piano, a trumpet can play only one note at a time. So it would take something like a brass band to produce sustained notes and harmony at the same time. Bowed strings can sustain beautifully as well, so a string quartet could also achieve the effect, if more quietly, as could a number of other generally impractical possibilities for the regular musical life of a parish. There is, however, one easy solution to produce this capability that we will explore.

Why would the ability to sustain multiple notes at a consistent volume simultaneously matter? Because that, my friends, is the *only* thing that will get a large, shy group of strangers to sing together (at least in Western culture generally). Our ancestors solved this issue generations ago, and it's a solution that works without fail in ballparks, bars, and basilicas. I will demonstrate shortly, but first, let's examine why encouraging congregational singing should be a goal.

---

and pitch, are dissimilar.... Timbre depends primarily upon the frequency spectrum, although it also depends upon the sound pressure and the temporal characteristics of the sound." What I am calling "sustain" is one of those temporal characteristics and a part of what audio engineers call the "attack, sustain, decay, release envelope" of a note. However, I'm intentionally avoiding such technical discussion here.

Music and Meaning in the Mass

The Requirements of Congregational Song

If your choir's music conveys a message congruent with the beauty of the truths unfolding in the Mass, your next task is to ensure that you are not doing this as a private exercise. You are charged with raising the hearts of the whole congregation through encouraging their active participation in such moving and appropriate song. Not all musical responsibilities are shared with the congregation—some belong exclusively to skilled music ministers—but the faithful should be led into the parts of the Mass that are necessarily theirs, not hindered from participation in them.

The Second Vatican Council's Constitution on the Sacred Liturgy expresses this very directly:

> Liturgical worship is given a more noble form when the divine offices are celebrated solemnly in song, with the assistance of sacred ministers and the active participation of the people.[28]

The saints say the same. Pope Saint John Paul II emphasized the choir's importance both independently and as a leader of the singing of the faithful,[29] quoting the Instruction *Musicam Sacram*:

> The conciliar norms regarding the reform of the liturgy have given the choir's function greater prominence and importance. The choir is responsible for the correct performance of its part, according to different styles of song, and to help the faithful take an active part in the singing.[30]

---

[28] Second Vatican Council, Constitution on the Sacred Liturgy *Sacrosanctum Concilium* (December 4, 1963), no. 113.

[29] For the centenary of Pius X's Motu Propio *Tra le Sollecitudini* on Sacred Music, November 22, 2003.

[30] Second Vatican Council, Instruction on Music in the Liturgy *Musicam Sacram* (May 14, 1967), no 19, http://liturgyoffice.org.uk/Resources/Music/Musicam-Sacram.pdf.

Today, Pope Francis frequently reminds liturgical musicians of this responsibility. At the third International Meeting of Choirs, he admonished:

> You are the musical animators of the whole congregation. Don't take its place, depriving the people of God of the chance to sing with you and bear witness to the Church's communal prayer.

There is a profound difference between observation and participation. Later in this book, when the musical implications of each part of the Mass are explored individually, it will become more and more clear how, through their prayerful engagement, the faithful either take part in critical actions that console the Heart of Jesus on the altar, or they don't. The second option is a tragedy.

However, it is the second option we encourage when we make it difficult to participate in sung responses. We as musicians might be doing this quite unwittingly through instrumental choices that can accidentally indicate that those there to participate should just sit quietly. A previous chapter explored how powerfully people respond to the external cues they are given and how hesitant we are to take any individual action in a group. Therefore, if we give a congregation indicators that say, "Do nothing," we know with near certainty that they will do nothing.

Many Catholics experience an almost visceral lament that we hardly sing together in church anymore. They remember the responses and hymns of their childhood fondly and even absorbed some of their own primordial catechesis from their participation in that music, ingrained in their hearts from the very act of joining in song. If we lament this, then it is incongruous to think that the problem is that those active Catholics who defy the prevailing culture and do come to Mass are then too disengaged to sing once they are there!

Music and Meaning in the Mass

They are not, and yet it is easy to think so from the position of the choir. Many a brave cantor has stood up in front of a congregation, smiled encouragingly, told everyone exactly where to find their music, and made the "let's all sing now" gesture of lifting his hand, only to be met with blank stares in response. It's a hurtful position of apparent rejection for the cantor.

What if, however, the smile, the page number, and the hand gesture, reasonable as they seem and good as they are, aren't the most important external cues people need to be able to sing? If they are not, what are the necessary cues? Let's look to our experience elsewhere.

We all can call to mind powerful moments of singing in large groups. In fact, one author suggests that our neurobiology is profoundly programmed to respond with enormous attachment to experiences of communal song. Further, he even asserts that the human propensity to do this is what allowed for the development of civilization.[31]

I agree! It's hard to imagine any way that we in earlier times could have built the Hebrew temple or sailed the Atlantic or marched to war or even met the person we would marry without the powerful bond of communal song. It seems a very essential part of our humanity as creatures who seek to transcend our individual purposes for a greater one. Therefore, as grace builds on nature, I believe shared music is also one of the most fundamental means God has given us to express our longing and love for Him.

In fact, when we think of ancient worship, it is hard to imagine it without communal song. We know King David wrote the psalms[32]

---

[31] I am thinking of a book called *The World in Six Songs* by Daniel Levitin, which became a *New York Times* best seller.

[32] The common understanding is that David is the author of Psalms, while some scholarship disputes that claim.

and Our Lord sang them! What other model do we need to show us that sung prayer is critical to God's plan for our worship?

Still, today we maintain mousy silence, trying to avoid eye contact with the urgently gesturing cantor. In doing so, we are depriving our faith of one of its greatest natural nourishments. Yet, we will sing and be deeply moved by doing so in far less important contexts. Why?

I admit getting teary-eyed when I remember the football games of my university days. Honestly, I can't recall who won or lost most of them. What I do remember is what would happen at the end, regardless of the outcome.

A clarion note would sound, and we would throw our arms over the shoulders of whoever might be to our left and our right. Then, swaying together with the music, close to a hundred thousand people would sing out in roaring unison, "Notre Dame our Mother, tender, strong, and true. Proudly in the heavens gleam thy gold and blue ..."

Those thousands of students are probably now the same people who won't utter a peep from the pew. Is it really that they care more about football than God and are therefore willing to sing for one and not the other? I'm sure that might hold for a few of us, but I contend that there is something else at play.

In the stadium, everybody was given the notes to the tune, and those notes were clearly sustained in a tonal color too bold to be ignored. The pitches didn't last for just a moment, their fleeting cues not meant to be caught by anyone who wasn't both attentive and musically inclined. No, we could find our notes if we didn't know them on our own, or if we missed the right moment to come in, or even if we had a beer during the game.

Melody was made so primary (and the music otherwise so properly ordered) that there was literally a marching band blaring each individual tone at you. It would take more effort to miss the right note than to find it. In those circumstances, everyone can have the utter confidence to sing.

Music and Meaning in the Mass

I suspect that's why there are bands at both football games and military events, since both can involve enormous crowds. Brass bands employ instruments whose timbre is loud, bright, and sustained, and these characteristics inspire confidence in nonprofessional large-group singing.

Have you ever heard a group of sleep-deprived, storm-weary sailors belt out "Anchors Aweigh"? All it takes is handing them their notes securely, and even the least musical sailor among them will deliver with the kind of moving gusto that demands that tissues be passed around.

Of course, additional group singing follows both football games and ships' returns. It takes place as these large gatherings disperse out to eating and drinking establishments. Not every song that comes over the sound system, however, gets everyone singing.

Unfailingly, one does. Even if he's not a favorite of a reveler's particular generation, people always sing a Neil Diamond song together. It's not even the whole song that they sing, but just a bit of the chorus. Can you hear it in your head?

People stop their conversations when they hear the words "Sweet Caroline," then, everyone together—waitstaff, revelers, and dishwashers included—belts out "BA-BA-BA!" Why do people always sing "BA-BA-BA"? Those aren't even words! They certainly can't bear special meaning that exceeds even the faith of most.

Can you see where this is going? It's not that they care particularly about three nonsense syllables. They do it because of the timbre of the instrument that plays the notes! It sets the stage for easy participation.

So, if we want to encourage participation, we have to use instruments with the right timbre. However, neither a brass band nor one like Neil Diamond's is a practical solution in a parish. For one among many reasons, such bands take too many people with too much varied and highly specific training to construct reliably.

For another, they would be too loud for all but the biggest church buildings and thus seem a little silly.

If only there was an instrument with strong sustain and a bold tonal character that worked in large crowds, but not stadium or aircraft-carrier-size crowds. An instrument that could manage harmony like a band but could be played by just one person. Something like the solution that has gotten minor-league-baseball-size crowds singing for generations. Hmmm.

Ideally, even if the instrument had an unlimited potential for mastery, it should not be too difficult to learn, so that it could be played by a determined high schooler or a retiree with a little time to practice at your parish. Even more ideally, it should cost many parishes nothing. And it doesn't, of course, because they already own it.

It's an organ. It's abandoned, and yet it need not be. The same person who is playing the electric piano near the altar can probably manage those same notes on the organ to enormous effect. Watch the hearts of your song-starved congregation leap when you try it. Better than that, listen to them sing!

Perhaps for reasons other than its ideal functionality, you remain organ averse, or perhaps for financial, architectural, or other concerns at your parish, an organ is an impossibility. It is important, then, to examine the alternatives. I will address those most common in American parishes, guitars and pianos, but many of the same thoughts apply to any instruments that similarly lack sustain.

Capabilities and Limitations of the Guitar

No words I can write will adequately express my love of the guitar or my sense of wonder at its capacity as an instrument. I will use the observation of Andrés Segovia instead. He is reported to have said, "The guitar is an orchestra, merely seen through the wrong end of an opera glass."

He was right. Few instruments (the organ being the second obvious possibility) give one player the potential to create the effect of an orchestra in microcosm. The guitar is capable of play-ing various combinations of rhythm, harmony, bass, and multiple melodies, all with different tonal colors—and all with rich and wildly expressive beauty.

As a rule, however, we typically do something very strange with this astounding instrument. We use it in a way equivalent to asking Julia Child to stop puttering around the kitchen and pick up some takeout for us. Or maybe using an iPhone as a hammer is a better analogy. How?

Whether we play in Segovia's style or simply play well at what-ever level our mastery allows, the capacities of the guitar are pro-duced by using our fingers to play the notes. That's reasonable, right? More often than not, however, we completely occupy the fingers of the right hand with holding a pick (a plastic imitation fingertip—so we already have several better models naturally attached).

With the pick, we strike the strings of the guitar in a single large gesture that could have been ten or twenty individual, meaningful notes instead. It is quite the same as a piano player using one hand to hold a brick while playing. The only thing he could do with the brick is use it to slam upon blocks of multiple notes at once.

In short, we strum chords, and we create a situation in which we can *only* strum chords. This limitation makes the guitar behave as a different kind of instrument than it really is. Used this way, the guitar is primarily a rhythm instrument (think: "strum, strum, strum, strum") and secondarily one that plays a part in harmony (we strum chords, as opposed to merely keeping a drumbeat).

What's the problem for congregational singing here? The gui-tar used in this way does not produce melody. Large groups of nonprofessionals need to hear the tune of the line they are expected to sing, clear and boldly sustained, in order to sing along.

"Wait," you might think, "my favorite band strums and sings along with the guitar, and it works fine!" Yes, it works wonderfully as a *performance* you are meant to *listen* to, and perhaps you, being musically talented, sing along with it alone. Your favorite band is made up of professionals who wrote the song themselves or know it intimately, not people trying to "pick it up." They are bandmates who practice it together regularly. With rare exceptions,[33] your congregation is none of those things.

Your favorite guitar band's instrumentation necessitates that their singing function as the melodic line. Your goal as the musical animator of a congregation is to get the congregation to take the melodic line. However, because the guitar doesn't play a bright, sustained melodic line and therefore demands that you sing "lead," it cues the congregation not to take the line away from you. This conspires with social programming that tells us not to interrupt a person's lead any more than we would chime in during Father's homily.

We frequently hear admonishments against liturgical musicians' "performing" or being somehow uninviting of the congregation's participation. Even the Holy Father's statement opening this chapter had a tone of warning—as if taking the liturgical responses

---

[33] The exception to this is in very small groups where both the music and the participants are extremely familiar, to the point that their secure friendship allows them to take the melodic line away from an apparent soloist. This exception would additionally have to take place in a small space lacking the acoustics of a typical church (e.g., you belong to a very tiny religious community, your chapel is the size of a living room, you sing the same music every day, and you know for certain that Sister Mary Perpetua doesn't mind when you join in).

away from the people was a secret temptation of the choir, against which they should guard themselves. Perhaps this is true of a very few musicians, but I don't think that the typical choir strumming through Mass is *trying* to prevent the congregation from singing.

I think our choirs are, in fact, trying their hardest to execute a difficult task for the love of God and also wonder why they are singing alone. I've seen dismay on the face of many cantors and directors as no one joins them. They deserve no blame.

They do deserve to understand *why* their musical approach is having the effect of silencing others. If they wish it to be different, they deserve to be offered the technical tools that will reverse that effect. Those understandings and options are what I seek to offer next.

Effects of Guitar Technique

I think neither the choir nor the ones criticizing their apparent performance orientation understand the technical realities of *why* strummed guitars have the effect they do. Without this understanding, our discussion soon becomes a battle over the wrong things—one of perhaps culture or taste or generation rather than the sort of dispassionate functional exploration it should be, much like why one drill bit is good for one task and another is good for another. Let's return to *that* discussion and make the answers available.

We've explored how a pick makes a guitar into a rhythm instrument. Now, even if you loved your guitar as much as I do, abandoned the pick, and faithfully utilized your instrument's capacity to create melody, that melody wouldn't have sustain. The guitar goes "pling" when it's plucked. Unlike instruments that use bows or air or other means for sustain, it has no capacity to go pliiiiiiiiiiiiiiiiing.

You could solve that problem by using a tremolo (in the classical sense of the technique—meaning hundreds of plings in quick succession) to create the illusion of sustained melody (plingingingingingingng). You'd get an A for creativity and effort in my book, but your brilliance would do you little good. Not a soul could hear that kind of delicacy over anyone trying to sing in a church.

Anthony Esolen is one of the few voices to address this issue from a lens of functionality rather than taste. He says:

> Why should the organ be the premier instrument for congregational singing? Can't a piano or a guitar work as well? No, they can't. The reasons are obvious. Around that camp fire, you want the guitar and not the organ. You're singing folk songs, everybody is within a few feet of you, and so it's not hard to pick up the tune and find your note: it's what Joe is singing right next to you, or what Melanie is singing on the other side of the fire.
>
> But in church this doesn't happen. The interior space is far too big, and the acoustics turn guitar-chords to mud. It won't help if the guitarist is miked up, for then it will be loud mud. But even if it weren't so, the guitarist is ill-suited to lead the congregation, because he is *not playing the melody*. He's playing chords; he makes a lead soloist necessary. So once again we are in the realm of a vocal performance, with all the troubles that entails.[34]

There's a problem even greater than this, and it goes back to something far more essential to what music communicates. Remember the first chapter's examination of melody, harmony, and

[34] Anthony Esolen, "Why Traditional Hymns are Superior to Modern Ones," *Crisis Magazine*, December 11, 2018, https://www.crisismagazine.com/2018/why-traditional-hymns-are-superior-to-modern-ones.

Music and Meaning in the Mass

rhythm? They each impact our intellect, emotions, and bodily impulses respectively. In all music, but especially in the context of the Mass, they must be ordered in this ranked prioritization, or what is communicated will, naturally, be disordered.

Imagine this scenario. A singer gets up to lead. For our made-up example, let's say her text is from Psalm 51: "Have mercy, O God, in your kindness. In your compassion blot out my offense."

You're the guitar player, and it's your job to accompany this. So, when the singer starts singing, you do what you do and strum a chord. It sounds like "brrrrum." So far, so good.

However, the "brrrrum" ends, and she's still singing. She has gotten only to "mercy," and all you're giving her is dead air. In the silence, maybe she's even becoming unsure of her pitch. Nobody wants dead, silent air, and nobody in the congregation is helping her sing, so it's your job to do something.

However, the only thing you can do is strum some more. You can go up or down with your pick. Since it's at the bottom of the strings now, you come back up, but there's dead air again, so you go back down, and so forth.

"Bruuum-ba-rrrrum-ba, bruuum-ba-rrrrum-ba, bruuum-ba-rrrrum-ba, bruuum-ba-rrrrum-ba ..." Now you're filling up the dead air, but to do it, you've just created a rhythm. A very dominating one, actually.

Maybe you're even more creative. You've played guitar enough in bands to know a few rhythms to try. You do something syncopated and catchy. "Brrrrom-ba-chinka-chinka-broom," maybe? You're getting into it now.

But what is she singing? Now she's at "My sacrifice a contrite spirit. A humbled contrite heart you will not spurn ... ba-chinka-chinka-broom."

We know the music has begun to, in its own language, say something incompatible with the meanings of the moment and of

70

the text. However, it has even gone so far as to become disordered. Rhythm has become its most predominant quality.

The guitarist doesn't mean to do this, but the way the instrument is used makes this the only possible outcome. No one sings with the cantor, and no one is able to absorb the text well when it is so simultaneously contradicted. At best, what could have moved hearts becomes merely an awkward moment we all need to "get through"—musicians and congregation included—all sensing things are wrong and no one knowing why. After all, the guitarist and vocalist both did their jobs.

Best Use of Guitar Technique

What can you do, however, if guitars (and similar instruments) are your only option? The organ is broken beyond repair, and your parish is poor. Perhaps you are truly in the position that gave rise to the beautiful carol "Silent Night"—when a rural parish's organ was ruined on Christmas Eve and the choirmaster responded with a stroke of inspired genius. The enduring beauty of a Mass accompanied by a single guitar that was achieved on that night should give you hope.

Or, less poetically but more probably, you are a music minister at something like a university dorm's chapel or at a far-flung military installation. A guitar is truly the only instrument at your disposal. By incorporating the principles we have examined so far, as much as possible in your circumstances, you can still make your music more fitting to the liturgy and more welcoming to congregational song.

In that situation, do what the composer of "Silent Night" undoubtedly did. I imagine he sang a steady, sustained melodic line[35]

---

[35] Another word for this is *legato*. "Siiiiiiileeent niiight," as opposed to "Si-i-lent night." Its importance is addressed further in the section to follow on "The Voice as an Instrument."

and arpeggiated his chordal accompaniment so that it would be less harshly rhythmic and at least present a more continuous impression to hearers. God gave us right hands with many fingers, and yet we use them all to hold a single pick? Why not use those fingers each to play a note?

A single arpeggiated chord is what made me fall in love with music as a tiny child. Surely the same can happen for you. I remember the day my young mom, a glamorously beautiful child of the '60s, fresh from San Francisco and popular with bands there (she was a lyricist for the Moby Grape), sat me down on the front porch and showed me her guitar.

She played a chord like an angel playing a harp—evenly and beautifully, with one finger to pluck each note. Mesmerized, I repeated "Ooooh, do it again! Do it again!" She obliged and increased my fascination until she finally responded "No, now you do it." That was all it took for me to want to accomplish nothing more.

You are many orders of magnitude smarter and more capable than a three-year-old, so I now issue you the invitation my mom issued to me. It is the one that started my life of music and opened my heart to the beauty that directed me to God. "You do it."

Someone reading this is saying "Oh no, that's fingerstyle! Or even worse, classical technique! I don't play like that!" Why not? Again, the requirement for technical proficiency in the Mass is not out of the range of a serious beginner.

Are you serious? I bet you are. You realize that the music of the Mass is critical to the salvation of souls and essential to the consolation of the Heart of Jesus on the altar. You are as serious as a heart attack.

Are you a beginner? I bet not. I bet you have been playing for a long while—perhaps many years—before reading this book.

So, sit down with an online video or a knowledgeable friend, and with the metronome and recorder that's likely on your phone, and learn to arpeggiate your chords. How many opportunities do you have to give a gift of effort so directly to Jesus as that? I pray that God rewards you enormously for it!

Capabilities and Limitations of the Piano

So much attention has been given to guitars here that it might seem that pianos are neglected. In fact, though, everything that has already been said about instruments whose tone lacks sustain applies. Whereas a guitar goes "pling," a piano goes "plink." There's not much difference on that front.

Pianists are less tempted to play rhythm exclusively, so that's an improvement over most guitar accompaniments. As a pianist, after reading this, you may be even more inclined to ensure that the elements of your accompaniment are properly ordered and give melody all the weight, reinforcement, and primacy you can for the sake of the congregation.

If a piano is your only option, this will go a long way. However, the real problem with the piano is the fact that if you are trained and talented enough on the keyboard to be playing it, you aren't using those abilities on the organ instead. If you're a keyboardist, and an organ is potentially available to you, I issue you an invitation as well.

For the sake of Jesus on the altar and for the sake of souls, I ask you to make an effort that's mildly arduous but not beyond you. Work to transition your skills to the organ. You don't need the proficiency of a master's degree in it to have a truly masterful impact with it.

The Voice as an Instrument

While we are exploring circumstances in which there may be no organ, let's also address circumstances in which there may be no instruments at all besides your voice and the voices of your congregants. If you are thoughtful and self-reflective about the basic principles that should apply, this is potentially one of the most beautiful circumstances in which music can accompany the liturgy. After all, the absence of instruments altogether completely avoids the potential disorder that can arise from arrangements not perfectly suited to the liturgy.

When I say this can be among the most beautiful circumstances for liturgical music, I don't mean to refer to anything necessitating the assembled training and precision of, say, a traditional unaccompanied Latin or Eastern choir. If you happen to have such music at your parish, praise God, you have no need of this book! You are employing the wisdom of generations of faithful who thoughtfully crafted beautiful solutions to every question this book explores—the very issues that we who abandon such music must try to solve alone and anew.

I am not attempting to address such specialized choirs here but instead the person who feels called to music ministry at the typical American parish. Perhaps you are unsure of your voice. Out of reverence, now understanding the weight and dignity of what music at Mass is meant to accomplish, you doubt if you could lead a congregation to experience the beauty of the Mass if it were all up to your voice alone. I want to assure you through an example.

During daily Mass at my parish, there is no one to lead the music but the pastor. I don't suspect he has much formal musical training, though he does have a sure basic sense of vocal technique. With only this, some of the most beautiful and effective congregational singing I've ever been a part of happens because of him. Why?

First, he has the qualities that the self-reflective practice I discuss in earlier chapters is meant to instill. For the sake of the beauty of the Mass, he won't tolerate himself to be wrong about notes (sharp or flat, early or late) or to sing with an unpleasing tone or a meaningless line. Second, he chooses to sing within the most natural and central part of his voice, which makes singing along natural for others as well. (This is a quality to be addressed in the next section.)

Third, and very critically, he sings a sustained melodic line. That means that his singing, as far as possible, imitates the way an organ or a trumpet creates continuous pitches, with each syllable held out for the full length of its value, rather than clipping his words as we do when we speak. This makes him easy to follow, as it keeps the melody dominant and clear.

For example, he might sing "Iiimmaaacuuulaaate Maaary," rather than allowing the quick decay of syllables and, thus, pitches in "I-mma-cu-late Ma-ry." The first might not sound as natural as the individualistic interpretations based on speech that are popular in music today. It sounds a bit more classical, and it takes more effort with one's breath, but it's much easier for others to sing along with if there is no other instrument offering a melody.

Finally, he chooses only very meaningful melodies with which our congregation is already familiar. They are often melodies that we who have Hispanic cultural roots will remember from childhood. This is necessary, given that there are no additional sustaining instruments to lead us, so we are limited in the ability to "pick up" anything new spontaneously.

What has happened since he arrived? Everyone began to sing out at daily Mass. Now the group even breaks out in beautiful harmonies from the pews!

Can you do more as a music minister than a singular priest can at daily Mass? Absolutely. However, by using the simple principles here for the barest circumstances, you know at least that you will now never do less than what is already beautiful and effective.

Swift Remedies for Congregational Singing

Everything I suggested so far is attainable within a reasonably short time for your choir. If you are as enthused as I am about changes we can make to console Jesus on the altar immediately, there remain a few quick suggestions for you to further your congregation's willingness to sing. These are things that you can address at your very next rehearsal and implement at your next Mass.

Range

An old joke asks how to know if there is a singer at the door. You will hear her struggling outside, because a singer can never find the right key. Finding the right key, however, presents an even easier and quicker fix to encouraging congregational singing than addressing instrumentation, and this is something your choir can remedy immediately.

Choir directors, I plead with you, even if you or your members have very unique professional voices with exceptionally high or low ranges, if the piece is meant to include the congregation, select a key best suited to average these extremes.[36] The rule at one time when writing music for group participation was to "keep it on the staff"—meaning select a key that would generally keep the melody from using notes higher or lower than those that fit within the treble clef lines (presuming that men would sing an octave below what is written). Current hymnals seem generally to adhere to this rule.

Today I think this is overly ambitious, unless and until a slightly more classicized method of singing comes into popular

---

[36] It should go without saying, but we have all witnessed the need to express it anyway, that if your choir does not possess the ability to reach certain notes reliably and beautifully, please do not choose keys that require them to attempt those notes during the Mass.

use again — one that emphasizes melody over spoken rhythm. Our glamorous grandmas sang rangy, arching melodies like Audrey Hepburn's "Moon River" from *Breakfast at Tiffany's* while flitting around the house. Our moms rocked righteously to "Unchained Melody."

We, on the other hand, chant almost single-note "songs" like "I'm Too Sexy for My Shirt" while pounding out a run on a treadmill. (This has all sorts of implications! Our society as a whole has begun to prioritize rhythm, which appeals to our lowest natural faculties, over melody, which appeals to our highest. This unprecedented fact warrants serious reflection.)[37]

Still, regardless of the reason, most members of a congregation will not typically reach for an F or an E at the top of the staff in their daily lives. That means, if a key isn't thoughtfully selected, the highest point of a congregational song may well be on a note that most people will be afraid to attempt. After the inability to identify the necessary notes, nothing will discourage participation so much as the fear of publicly cracking one's voice on a note that is too high, particularly at a very noticeable moment. People will remain silent rather than take that risk.

Alternately, people are not nearly as afraid of a line including a note that is too low, as less public embarrassment is involved. In a group, low notes, whether they are good or bad, are far less audible. (This is not to encourage decentralizing melodies toward the lowest tessitura or average pitch, as aiming too low in this sense makes everything consistently harder to hear and works against congregational singing as well.)

[37] It represents a call to Catholic musicians to exercise the powerfully influential beauty of their consciously well-ordered art outside the liturgy as well, but that's beyond the scope of the discussion here. Nothing can influence the world so much as the Mass, so music outside of it is a secondary concern.

Therefore, I suggest another simple rule of thumb. Try to select a key that keeps the melody around the range between middle C and the C an octave above (or maybe D, if you know your congregation's capabilities well enough) and aim for as much centrality in that range as possible. To remember it, just recall that your congregation thrives "from C to shining C."

If a song cannot fit quite neatly within an octave, it's probably a bad choice for congregational participation. If it's beautiful and necessary, assign it to a singer when congregational participation isn't required or expected, as in the meditation period following Communion. Such a song should be assigned only to a singer or singers who truly meet the basic requirements of individual proficiency outlined in chapter 3.

Tempo

Another quick fix that can make congregational singing feel more welcoming to participants is to take a moment to examine your approach to tempo. What determines how fast or slow a song should go? The meaning of the piece alone should dictate this.

That is to say, a piece of music that expresses excitement and hope should move at a brisker pace than one that expresses lament or despair. "Joy to the World" could bound along exultantly. "By the Cross Her Station Keeping" should move with mournful reverence. Few are the pieces that should belong to either extreme.

I mention this because it often seems our tempi are determined by factors other than meaning. Catholic choirs have somewhat fairly earned a reputation for singing everything at the tempo of a dirge. I suspect this may have, at one point, reflected a lack of technical proficiency.

We might initially approach an unfamiliar piece by going very slowly to ensure that everyone is able to keep up with necessary chord changes and other demands. However, even when we have gained familiarity, the tempo can remain as part of an unintentional habit. The minor suggestions in chapter 3 for improving technical proficiency and breaking out of unhelpful musical habits should easily resolve this.

We might also hear choirs that do things too fast. This can be caused by anything from anxious nerves to the influence of upbeat dance rhythms. If that's the case, hopefully this book thus far has helped you determine when and whether such rhythms have a place in the solemn responses of the Mass. If not, the final chapter will investigate more deeply exactly what each response requires in order for its meaning to be well expressed in music of any style.

On that note, before moving on from these general technical topics, let us be reminded to let the music's meaning govern not just tempo but every interpretational choice we make, insofar as our goal remains always to speak truth with music. Let's aim not merely to succeed in playing or singing the notes but to make meaningful statements out of them. To invite your congregation into song is to invite them into active participation in the breathtaking mysteries of the Mass moment by moment, at each point of its unfolding. Those moments are what we will explore next.

5

A Musician's Call to Mysticism

An astounding fact bears reflection here. In the Mass, we experience the reality for which the mystic heart longs — real union with our God. However, we receive such grace only in the degree to which our souls are disposed to accept it.[38]

When your music at Mass influences the readiness of our souls, by stirring within us a deeper grasp of what is taking place on the altar, your welcoming of Our Lord in the Blessed Sacrament has glorious repercussions! Imagine the increase in His grace that could be poured out on the whole world through those souls your music prepares to receive Him with love! It is, after all, through His action in our souls — through the making of saints — that God changes the world!

Because of this, my musical friends, it is no exaggeration to say that you are in the business of making saints. To do it, you are called

---

[38] Jesus is always truly physically and completely present in the Eucharist, regardless of our recognition or response. However, how deeply He is welcomed in our souls and how much we permit Him to remain in us with His grace and transform us depends on our preparedness and "disposition," or the degree of our inclination to desire Him. These are things on which your music can exert a profound influence.

to be a special kind of saint as well. By exploring the musical parts of the Mass, the next chapter will help you learn, like a mountain guide, like the trumpeter before an army, the paths along which your special vocation as a liturgical musician invites you to lead others.

Much as the Real Presence in the Eucharist is rarely understood among today's Catholics and the role of the musician is essential to restoring our experience of it, perhaps even more rarely understood is the life of the soul itself—a life that can be roused and nourished through music, especially in the pinnacle of our encounter with God in the Mass. The Mass is the only real and eternally meaningful epic, operatic, cinematic drama there is, and the individual soul has a leading role. Everything lies in balance with each soul's relationship to Jesus on the altar.

If you are a liturgical musician, this goes a step further. *Other* souls are profoundly influenced by *your* role in the drama of this relationship as it is expressed in your art. For this reason, I argue that if you are a musician, you are uniquely called to be a mystic in the true and ancient Catholic sense of the word.[39] That is, you must be particularly awakened among your peers to the life of your soul and respond with love and longing to God's invitation to intimacy in order to communicate that invitation to others.

---

[39] I suspect, musical friend, that upon reading those words, you already know that they are true. You already speak a language of love in your music, and you direct it toward God. Don't be misled, however, by modern misuses of the word "mystic," which associate it with a faithless fascination with the supernatural. No, the mystical tradition of the Catholic Church is one in which a soul's entire focus is on an ever-deepening loving relationship with God. This chapter will help explain. However, it's better to read some lives of great mystic saints, such as Saint Teresa of Avila, Saint John of the Cross, Saint Thérèse of Lisieux, Saint Edith Stein, or the great Padre Pio, for real inspiration and to learn how the life of prayer follows the paths of the Mass.

Pushing aside the long mystical wisdom of the Church, it seems that today we've begun to treat the eternal fate of our souls as a pass-or-fail issue. That is, in the end, we either make it to Heaven or go to Hell; and since, when we look around us, few people seem bad enough to deserve Hell in our opinions, we are content to think that we, along with them, are probably going to make it to Heaven eventually. Tragically, our eternal aspirations can end there.

Certainly making it to Heaven is better than not! However, this reduction forgets that the goal of our souls, Heaven itself, is a *relationship* with God, not some sort of physical destination where arriving is the end. Heaven is not a magnificent tourist spot like the Grand Canyon where, if you make the trip, you get to enjoy the same view as anyone else who does the same.

I recently attended the eightieth birthday party of a famous artist and wildly colorful Navy veteran much beloved by our community. The food was delicious, the laughter was contagious, and the house was a glowingly warm refuge from the drizzly winter outside. Everyone there enjoyed these things.

In fact, the birthday girl was such a popular figure in town and her liberal hospitality was so well known that the party was huge! People were there who knew her only distantly. Nephews and second cousins and out-of-town in-laws of her friends were there, and they were all imminently welcome.

However, the food, the warmth, and the welcoming atmosphere weren't the point of the party. The point was to celebrate and to spend time with the birthday girl, and those who knew her best got to enjoy it the most. Those who had shared experiences with her could laugh more heartily at inside jokes. Those who were genuinely thrilled at her accomplishments and were, in some little way, a part of them, had a level of enjoyment of her successes.

What's my point? While a generous acquaintance might invite you into his or her house, there is a world of difference between spending time with an acquaintance and a friend, and the closer and dearer the friendship, the more meaningful and enjoyable nearness to that person becomes. So, mystics throughout the ages of the Church have reminded us that our goal in the spiritual life isn't just to arrive at the party but to know the host as intimately as possible!

They teach us, therefore, that there are degrees of relationship with God, and every soul is meant for a journey of ever-growing relationship with Him through phases of increasing intimacy. The gift of the Church's great mystic doctors is a map of these phases.[40] Though God can do anything (such as blinding Saint Paul in a brilliant burst of self-revelation and effecting an instant conversion), He typically leads souls toward a deep relationship with Him through the degrees of a journey — usually akin to a climb.[41]

Because these Church teachings are hardly ever emphasized in my generation — a loss almost as profound as our lack of understanding of the Mass — many souls today tragically lack a map for the journey they are meant to take. These souls are like sailboats built for offshore ocean racing docked on an inland lake, and no one ever shows them there's a salty sea to reach. They do not know it exists, and so it does not figure in their hopes or dreams, and they pass into eternity without ever achieving the glorious end for which they were built.

[40] I am, of course, thinking of the Doctors of the Church Saint John of the Cross and Saint Teresa of Avila, in works like *The Ascent of Mount Carmel* and *The Interior Castle*, as well as the works of their spiritual children over the ages, where God's map for the soul who seeks Him, revealed in Scripture, is laid out through the teaching of those with profound experience.

[41] Thus Saint John's mountain, Saint Teresa's castle, and Saint Thérèse's staircase and elevator analogies.

They may be saved, but the truth they are never told is that they were created and called to become great saints — souls who, by constantly striving to respond to and cooperate with the graces extended to them, pursued a close relationship with God in this life. Great saints enjoy Heaven and draw others toward Heaven with them in a way that souls who, believing that Heaven is merely a destination that they'll likely reach in the end, cannot. By the mercy of God, dispassionate souls may "make it" to Heaven, but because they never desired to know their Host well or intimately, they may enjoy it only as much as a guest on the outer edges of a party can.[42]

What a loss! Its tragedy is compounded by its irrevocability, as this life alone is our chance to develop and express that desire for intimacy in the darkness of faith that proves our love and to take the adventurous and dramatic ascending mystic journey toward God's love that He holds out to us! We will realize this at our deaths and then, if destined for Heaven, long to love Him because we will have seen Him unveiled; but those who desired to embark upon the climb in this life will have pursued a different kind friendship from those who never thought of it.

This is, incidentally, one reason why cutting short the full natural course of any human life is such an intolerable heartbreak in the Catholic worldview. Every moment one is alive is a new chance

---

[42] They will not fail to enjoy it! They will merely be satisfied with the snacks. In her autobiography, Saint Thérèse took up this question when she wondered as a child about the human capacity for happiness. She came to the conclusion that all souls in Heaven are fully and completely happy, to the point of over-brimming. It's just that, like the glasses in her family's cupboard, some people's capacity for that happiness will be greater. Some will be full as thimbles and some will be full as goblets. This life is our sole chance to expand the capacity of our hearts by growing in love.

to grow in this relationship. Every moment discarded is an eternal forfeiture of a degree of love and joy a soul could have known in the next life and drawn others toward in this one.

Do we, who are alive now, take advantage? Does the art God has given us the talent to make encourage others to do so? Saint Teresa of Avila tells us that the difference in the degrees of Heaven is so great that when we die, we will realize we would have joyfully preferred to live through every torment of this world until its end just to attain one more minute step of closeness to God in eternity.[43]

How, then, do we pursue the relationship we are meant to have with God? If we're headed for Heaven, the only way there is by a steep climb, following our Lord to Calvary (Matthew 16:24). Fortunately, He leads us and His grace carries us along the way. So, why wait? Putting it off will never get us farther along!

The opportunity to climb toward Calvary is present in every struggle of our lives, and the literal ability to approach Calvary itself is present to us at every Mass! Progress in the spiritual life disposes the soul for greater union with God. The progression of the Mass should likewise dispose the soul for union with Christ in the Eucharist.

---

[43] This is from chapter 37 of her *Life*, titled "The Effects of the Divine Graces in the Soul. The Inestimable Greatness of One Degree of Glory."

6

The Mystic Design of Music in the Mass

Our role and response as musicians begins to emerge. How can souls be expected to get where they are meant to go when, especially today, no one speaks of the necessary directions or hints that we should even aspire to discover them? By the grace of God, my friends, the mystics' map is in the Mass! It can become more evident and influential if we musicians cultivate an intimate familiarity with the outline of its drama in order to underscore it in a way that emphasizes its meaning.

The map reveals three inspiring peaks, each loftier than the one before, and the summit of the third pierces the clouds and approaches the heavens.[44] If the idea calls to mind images out of Tolkien's *Lord of the Rings* or some other great saga, your artistic

---

[44] These "peaks" are usually referred to as the purgative, illuminative, and unitive stages, or the way of beginners, proficients, and the advanced, or simply spiritual childhood, adolescence, and adulthood—as the three "acts" of the drama follow a pattern imbued deeply with us, though today it goes ignored in many ways. There are two "valleys" between these great peaks, called by Saint John of the Cross the dark night of the spirit and the dark night of the soul, which render passage from one stage to the next, but because the Mass is a bird's eye view of the journey, it resembles a more continuous ascent.

imagination is in the right place. Music can communicate the drama of the soul's ascent toward God and lead souls along its paths, but in order for it to do so, musicians must understand how and where those peaks occur in the unfolding of the Mass.

In the first stage of the spiritual life, with God's grace, a soul begins its mystic journey and turns away from sin, just as we do in the Introductory Rites of the Mass. In the second part of the spiritual life, a soul grows in knowledge and understanding of God, just as we do in the Liturgy of the Word. In the third part of the spiritual life, the soul approaches true intimacy with God, just as we do in the Liturgy of the Eucharist. Finally, the soul returns to the world (if it does not pass into eternity) and brings God's love into it through the intimacy it has found, as occurs in the Concluding Rites.

What must you, as a musician, accomplish at each of these moments to usher our souls through? With your performance mastery and congregational leadership in place, the most fundamentally critical function you perform as a musical guide for souls in the Mass lies in the decisions you make. Like a briefing on the mystic terrain, this chapter presents the background you will need regarding each musical opportunity of the Mass in order to lead souls by your artistic choices.

Using This Chapter to Make Musical Decisions

This chapter seeks to empower you to make a good musical decision for any part of the Mass from among the myriad options available.[45] It will examine each frequently sung portion of the Mass, name each essential characteristic with which the music must comply,

---

[45] The same tools will help you compose, if you are so inclined and if no other setting quite meets the needs of your parish context.

and explain the reason why music occurs there and what sung prayer accomplishes in the unfolding drama of the Mass and the soul. This will make your decision easy.

All you must do, then, is ask, if your parish was watching a great cinematic epic in which a given moment occurred (e.g., a repentant sinner was welcomed to his father's table, the angels sang at Bethlehem, Christ entered Jerusalem in triumph — all of which we participate in throughout the Mass), would the soundtrack accompanying that moment be anything like the music you are considering and the way you plan to execute it? In short, play in your mind the "Jay Leno" scenario described earlier. If the answer is yes, your decision is made!

If the answer is no, and the issue is with the music itself, you can return to the tools in chapter 1 regarding the language of music (rhythm, harmony, and melody) to help you choose another song or setting that better "speaks" the truth of the moment you are try-ing to convey. (Or write one if you are so inclined!) If the answer is no and the issue is one of performance, the tools in chapters 3 and 4 will help with solutions.

Recall especially that your choice need not be ambitious or difficult to be right. First, it simply must not contradict the truth of the action that is unfolding. Second, it must advance it in the hearts of those present.

Music and Meaning in the Mass

Introductory Rites

The Entrance Song

Both the Mass and the spiritual life begin with a demarcation away from the world and the awareness of entering into a sacred realm where God is present. Achieving this demarcation is the first task of the parish musician in the entrance song. The song must spur the listener into recognizing that what is about to happen is entirely different from what happens in the world.

This is why a song that sounds no different from what might have been playing on the radio when a parishioner exited his car just a moment before doesn't help with the task. Ask yourself what you can do, within your choir's capabilities, to create that difference. Is it a question of instrumentation? Is it a question of rhythm?

Do people in your parish neighborhood love dancing the cumbia? This is the moment to do something very different from a cumbia. Whatever sounds "everyday" is the thing to avoid.

More important than "don't" suggestions, however, is what you can do to actively create a sacred atmosphere. If you are not relying on traditional resources, this will be different for every culture and every community. For example, where I grew up, many people would enjoy flamenco dancing on Saturday night.

I'll never forget the first Sunday of Lent one year when the entrance song, sung by the same people who performed at the flamenco show the night before, was accompanied only by a cane pounded on the floor at dramatic intervals. We joined in a Spanish hymn we all knew well, sung slower and with greater reverence than usual. It was *different*, and it filled me with the spine-tingling awareness that what was about to happen was different as well.[46]

---

[46] Similarly, consider how melodies we associate with Advent ("Let All Mortal Flesh Keep Silence," "Creator of the Stars of Night," and "O Come, O Come, Emmanuel") and Lent ("Attende,

This exit from the mundane (literally, that which is "of this world") and procession toward the holy (literally, that which is "other than") should begin and be sharply defined by the entrance song. However, the musical distinction you make here should last throughout the Mass. If your goal is dramatic continuity, your decision now will impact the entire liturgy.

Allow me to offer another example from my personal experience as a Hispanic Catholic, as I am certain it translates to every other parish's own culturally and situationally unique version of the same issue. Anyone who is as much a fan of mariachi and ranchero music as I am will know immediately what I am referring to, even though, without notation, it is a bit wordy to describe. There is a musical "tag" that we like to use to conclude songs in this style.

After the apparent end of anything in ¾ time, which is almost everything, we play a cheerful ascending four-note bass line, followed by the seventh chord and tonic. "Bum-bum-bum-bum! BA-DUM!"[47] It functions in much the same way as, and is even very musically reminiscent of, the barbershop quartet tag-on "Shave and a haircut, two bits!"

To finish with this ending is almost compulsive and unconscious. We learn it as children from our grandparents and probably never think about it again. It's "just how songs end." Instead, let's become conscious

---

Domine," "O Come and Mourn with Me Awhile," and "Stabat Mater") create a deep sense that these seasons are different from Ordinary Time. If you are not using these themes in your Advent and Lent liturgies, please try them out! They all work particularly well a capella or with minimal organ accompaniment.

[47] By the way, it's a fantastic thing that mariachi-style guitarists consistently demonstrate the skill to play an independent bass line! That's just what I talk about in chapter 4! Let's just not (myself included) use that skill to create this particular signal of the mundane. Let's get creative with the ability instead!

of the musical meaning of the messages we're sending. Abandoning it at the entrance song and leaving it off throughout Mass would go so far to communicate that what we are doing in the music at Mass is nothing like what we do with the music we create anywhere else.

Otherwise, imagine the things we hear! Later, Christ, the paschal Lamb, truly present, sheds His blood in sacrifice on the altar. We plead to Him directly: "Lamb of God, who takes away the sins of the world, grant us peace. Shave and a haircut, two bits." It might be tiny things like this that are screaming out to your parish that what is happening is mundane or simply can't be supernatural, or else we wouldn't treat it as we do.

Let the entrance song be the firm break from musical habits that belong elsewhere. It would take no more musical skill or practice, in fact less, but more understanding and reverence, simply to end the entrance song on a lingering and appropriate final chord than to add the tag unthinkingly. There may be those who argue, however, that to abandon such ingrained tendencies that form a characteristic part of the music of a particular culture is to work against liturgical enculturation and accessibility.

I would respond that such an argument does not give the depth of any culture's traditional music nearly enough credit. If music is a language, I trust its "speakers" in each parish to choose the terms that are appropriate, without cliché, to the expression of what is occurring at Mass. To reduce the essential characteristic of mariachi music, let's say, to an unconscious "BA-DUM," when it is capable of breaking hearts and lifting spirits in a myriad of ingenious ways, is a genuine insult.

This is an additional reason why, because I am writing for communities of every tradition and taste, I do not suggest what and how you should play.[48] Instead, I hope only to offer widely applicable

---

[48] Composing an easily played, accessible, and beautiful Mass that adheres to the principles I put forward here might be a next project

tools and insights to empower musicians to make appropriate musical decisions for the liturgy. I trust that my readers will, in the best way for their parishes, which only they know with the intimacy of members and leaders, use their unique talents and perspective to express effectively the truth of each moment of the Mass.

While the spiritual life begins with an entrance inward for the individual, the Mass begins with the gathering of a community, which embarks together with mutual support upon a pilgrim procession through life and up to the altar of Calvary (represented by the procession of the priests and servers, which the song accompanies). Therefore, besides encouraging an experience of separation from the world, the entrance song should help your congregation feel drawn together with one another.

Almost more than any other song you select, therefore, it should be familiar, be singable, and comply as much as possible with the other suggestions in the previous chapter for encouraging congregational participation. If you have an organ, this would be an excellent time to make even very simple use of it. Remember that singing as one binds groups together more closely than almost any other activity, and do everything you can to make this a moment in which people are compelled to join.

This is not just a good idea but a theological necessity. It is only with engaged and active, prayerful participation that anyone can experience or offer his or her part in the unfolding of the Mass. To sit for an hour without the least awareness of what is taking place is not participating. It is not taking the journey, receiving its graces, or consoling Jesus' Heart. It's making a park bench of a pew—a waste and a tragedy.

---

for me. I also advocate that you, as a parish musician, if you feel inspired, make it a project as well, speaking truth in a language that embraces your community's unique needs and tastes.

Music and Meaning in the Mass

The entrance song is your first and most powerful opportunity to draw congregants into that active participation. It's the salvo in your mission to reach their souls and the first clarion expression of your trumpet call, bidding us to holiness. Don't hold back here.

Reminders for the Entrance Song

- Here, you help your congregation leave behind the world and enter upon a sacred journey, unbound by our usual perceptions of time and space. You begin your role as a "mountain guide," if you will, along the mystic's map.
- To accomplish this, your music must be distinguishable from what is everyday or typical of the world your parishioners inhabit, which will differ depending on your context.
- Ask yourself how you can increase the sense of entering upon the otherworldly. Can you adjust tempo or dynamics and sing with more meaning? Can you use different instruments or play differently than you do in non-sacred settings? Can you choose a song that does not too closely resemble something your parishioners might hear outside of a sacred place?
- Be careful to identify "cues" related to the mundane that can unconsciously creep into your music (things that resemble "shave and a haircut, two bits" or "cha-cha-cha," from earlier examples) and leave them off throughout the Mass.

The Mystic Design of Music in the Mass

The Kyrie (Lord, Have Mercy)

After the decision to enter into the Mass or the spiritual life, both begin with a period of purgation—of spiritual cleansing. No one who is not in a state of grace, having confessed and been given sacramental absolution for any mortal sins, can receive Jesus in the Eucharist. However, even when we're not in any serious sin, we almost always come to Mass with some venial sins or imperfections, and these, too, make our souls inhospitable to Christ's presence.

So, souls who seek intimacy with Jesus, both on their mystic journey and in the Eucharist, must begin by identifying their sins and imperfections, feeling sorrow for them, and resolving to root them out. Those souls have decided, with God's grace, that they desire Jesus more than anything that draws them away from Him. We express this at Mass in the Confiteor ("I confess to almighty God ..."), and we seek God's mercy in the Kyrie.

To begin to understand what this music must convey, imagine Jesus coming physically to dwell within you. Imagine the perfect goodness of Mary, the worthy vessel in whom He dwelt first, and consider how vastly you and I differ from her. Think about whatever quality of hers moves you most—e.g., her gentle kindness versus our cruelty, her motherly warmth versus our cold neglect, her radiant purity versus our filth. What incredible mercy, then, would be necessary for Jesus to come to dwell in us?

How might we beg for it? How might we acknowledge it? How might we show awe-filled gratitude for the possibility of such inconceivable generosity reaching down to our souls?

If the music you are thinking of here sounds at all flippant or chipper, it's time to say bluntly that it's wrong. If you thought you were singing at this point to provide a bit of background, it's time to realize you're not. What you are doing is leading the congregation in prayer for this unimaginable mercy that we receive in order to proceed further in the Mass.

The faithful must be moved to repent and plead along with you, or their participation at this point will not be active, and the active preparation of their hearts, minds, and souls is essential to their worthy reception of Jesus. Imagine His sadness to be received into an unrepentant, unmoved, oblivious heart. Imagine the transformative gifts and graces that the soul who receives Him this way fails to accept, though Jesus offers them with wide-open arms. Does this further convince you of the critical nature and eternal consequence of your work?

Musical moods that might be appropriate for the Kyrie are stark, sorrowful, pleading, and humble. If you do not possess instruments that convey these feelings because of their more exuberant rhythmic tendencies, this might be the moment to sing unaccompanied, and allow your voice to do the imploring if the melody is haunting enough to convey the meaning. If you can manage appropriate instrumentation, almost certainly in a minor key[49] or a mournful mode and slow tempo, then offer it.

It is interesting that the Kyrie was the one part of the Latin Mass in which a prayer was retained in the more ancient Greek. The point of the prayer was understood regardless of the language. If you want to create a similar sense of distance from the mundane, you might retain or incorporate the original language as well.

Regardless of language, however, the setting and execution of the Kyrie must break hardened hearts. Besides the techniques already discussed, what else can you do so that the Kyrie will effectively lead the congregation to plead for and acknowledge this stunning gift of mercy? This moment is so crucial that I will offer an additional suggestion that makes musical expression more

---

[49] Key suggestions, here and throughout, assume a predominantly Western culture in your listeners.

meaningful and will act as an aid to your own spiritual life and that of the congregation you influence through your music.

Please consider creating a meditation every week that you pray about and allow to influence your thoughts and feelings when you sing the Kyrie. As appropriate to this moment in the Mass, it can be linked to your personal examination of conscience. For instance, this week, I am thinking about the crown of thorns, and the painful irony of the word "Lord," in "Lord, have mercy," when the torturous crown my sins have placed upon Jesus mocks His Lordship. There are an inexhaustible number of other meditations that might be meaningful to you.

Why do I do this? Even in secular music, our thoughts and feelings mysteriously unlock emotional understanding for the listener. When a musician is being taught interpretation at a conservatory, he or she might spend a year on a piece, being told to make a phrase louder here, softer there, held a bit longer here, and played with a bit more intensity there. There is a shortcut, however, to achieving most of this, and it is to assign a story to the music.

Professionally, I perform either as an instrumental soloist or in operas that are typically in a language foreign to the audience. That means that every bit of emotion I convey cannot be expressed through words. I must make people feel what the music is trying to say.

Therefore, I have spent endless hours coming up with stories for my instrumental music and subtexts for my operatic characters. I dream up tragic romances and great heroes and wild adventures at sea that I imagine intently while I perform so that the notes naturally conform to the nuances of my emotional state. In the end, when an audience is moved to intense emotion in response, it is because I have done *this* well, regardless of all the other technical work it may have taken not to detract from the story being told.

Unlike the drama that unfolds at a concert hall, of course, what takes place at Mass is *real* and of eternal consequence. However, if people can feel and respond to the emotion of a musician thinking of silly stories and are moved, how much more truly involved with the music's meaning will your congregation become if you make it your own heartfelt prayer, with a highly specific intent.

For instance, think through *why*, in the Kyrie, you are singing a similar phrase three times and why the difference occurs when there is one. "Lord, have mercy. Christ, have mercy. Lord, have mercy." Because this is a prayer, in our hearts and minds, we must have meaning and motivation for each phrase we sing.

The biblical motivations for threefold prayer will be discussed in a later section, as they increase in importance throughout the Mass. Notice, though, that in the Confiteor we repeat three times, "through my fault, through my fault, through my most grievous fault." The Kyrie then echoes this admission with a threefold cry for mercy.

I love an observation by Dr. Edward Sri, who remarks that when we say "I'm sorry," if we really mean to apologize and reconcile with someone we love and have committed some offense against, we hardly ever leave it at two words. Instead, we repeat it a few ways. "I'm so sorry I hurt you. That was cruel and selfish of me. I can't tell you how much I regret it."

As to lead a march, you must be marching, so to lead in prayer, you must be praying. To make listeners feel and understand this moment, you must feel and understand it first — and perhaps more deeply than those listening. Sing the Kyrie, my friends, in this way, and others will be led through the expression of your music into this prayer. At this and every stage, their full participation in the Mass leans upon your leadership.

Reminders for the Kyrie

• Jesus cannot enter and be welcomed into a sin-stained heart.[50] If we fail to feel or be reminded that we must turn away from our sins and ask forgiveness at this point in the Mass, we can more easily forget it is literally Jesus Himself we encounter later.

• You help your congregation to understand this by communicating feelings of sorrow, regret, repentance, and longing for mercy and reconciliation.

• Ask yourself if your music communicates these feelings in rhythm, harmony, and melody, and if it does not, choose a selection that does. (See additional notes pages 50–51.)

• Consider a slow tempo, a minor key, and stark instrumentation. Avoid peppy or bouncy rhythms. Most importantly, a beautiful, pleading melody delivered with your own prayerful intent of repentance will speak to your congregation's hearts.

• Remember that in coming face-to-face with the Eucharist, you come face-to-face with the very Person you will meet at your judgment. Plead for His mercy now as you will then, and you will not fail to move your congregation to do the same.

---

[50] If we have any unconfessed serious (mortal) sins, we must always receive sacramental absolution before we are able to receive Jesus in the Blessed Sacrament. To do otherwise is to commit an additional mortal sin of sacrilege. It is a failure to treat lovingly the gift of Love Himself.

Music and Meaning in the Mass

The Gloria (Glory to God in the Highest)

The Gloria celebrates the story of our salvation. It proclaims the entirety of what God has done for the world. Again, if you have ever wondered why you sing the words you sing here, now is the time to realize their function and make the prayer your own, so that your leadership draws others to participate.

Having received the mercy for which you plead in the Kyrie, the musical expression of the state of your prayer takes a dramatic shift. Musical moods that might be appropriate for the Gloria can be more diverse than what is appropriate for the Kyrie as long as they do not contradict the meanings of the sacred text. The prayer expresses, first, intense and joyful gratitude to God for His mercy by proclaiming His glory!

With regard to instrumentation, where the Kyrie was stark, the Gloria can be lush. With regard to rhythm and tempo, where the Kyrie was slow and mournful, the Gloria can move with excitement or remain stately with reverent awe. With regard to harmony and melody, the key for the Gloria can and will likely be major, but such a change cannot cause the music to become merely "cheerful" in its more trivial sense.[51]

Again, this isn't the time for a ditty; it is time to consider what glory might sound like! I imagine it's not so much common happiness as deep joy. Recall how time and space behave differently in the Mass and realize with whom you are singing. At this point, you unite your song with that of the angels when they announced Jesus' birth to the shepherds near Bethlehem.

---

[51] Also, this potential key change must not be jarring to the ear. Any complete Mass setting will ensure an appropriate transition, but if you are "cutting and pasting" pieces of different settings, this could be a concern. For this reason, and also for building continuity in the drama of the Mass, it is often better to use a complete setting that fulfills all the requirements for suitability.

Interestingly, biblical scholars tell us that the shepherds near Bethlehem were tasked with breeding spotless lambs for the Passover sacrifice.[52] When they found a perfect lamb, they wrapped it in swaddling clothes to keep it clean and laid it in a manger to keep it safe, so that not one of its bones would be broken (John 19:36). They did not, therefore, miss a nuance of the sacrificial drama that the angel's message about the child they found revealed.[53] You are proclaiming and making present the same drama to your congregation.

How might the angels have sung when they announced Jesus' birth to the shepherds with the words we hear at Christmas? "Glory to God in the Highest, and on earth, peace to people of good will!" (see Luke 2:14). If you can't imagine your music fitting that scene and harmonizing with the angels themselves, it is time to make a different musical choice.

Why does your congregation need to hear you sing, with the angels, the same announcement the shepherds heard in Bethlehem?

[52] This invites your own research, as the sources are many. Here, however, is a quick, accessible article mentioning the sheep bred specifically for sacrifice at Migdal Eder, just outside Nazareth: Joe Tremblay, "What You May Not Know about Christmas," Catholic News Agency, November 22, 2013, https://www.catholicnewsagency.com/column/what-you-may-not-know-about-christmas-2739. On the the use of swaddling clothes to preserve these lambs in an unblemished state, see Michael J. McCormick, "Wrapped in Swaddling Clothes and Lying in a Manger," Catholic365.com, December 16, 2018, http://www.catholic365.com/article/9662/wrapped-in-swaddling-clothes-and-lying-in-a-manger.html.

[53] I'm always awed by the way Scripture continually points to Jesus in the Eucharist, even in the tiniest details. He was laid in a manger? The word manger itself means "a place for eating." It is where animals were fed. He was born in Bethlehem? The town's name means "house of bread" in Hebrew and "house of flesh" in Arabic. It's hard to miss the critical, central message that Jesus' flesh is just what He says it is: "real food" (John 6:55).

It is because the very thing that happened to the shepherds is happening to them! In genuine reality, both announcements are equally monumental.

Like the shepherds, your congregation will see Jesus Himself, in the flesh. As a baby in Bethlehem, Jesus was tiny, vulnerable, poor, and while He could provoke our tender love, He perhaps even more easily provoked our coldness and confusion. How could this fragile little thing in unfortunate surroundings be our Savior, let alone God Himself?

How did the shepherds know they weren't merely visiting the squalid quarters of any homeless family with a newborn? It was the announcement of the angels that gave them the first means to understand the situation differently. Because of the music of the angels, they could instead marvel and offer Him their love.

As the Eucharist, Jesus is again present incarnate, and, like a poor baby, He is tiny and vulnerable. His glory is unrecognizable by human senses. So, again He easily provokes our coldness and confusion.

We, too, ask how this fragile thing could be our Savior, God Himself. In fact, too often we imagine He isn't. It is you, with the choirs of angels, who must sing in a way that allows us to feel the revelation so deeply that we, like the shepherds, may marvel and offer Him our love.

Time operates from God's perspective at Mass, not ours. All things are present to God at once. Christ's sacrifice is made present on the altar not because it is repeated but because it is the *same* sacrifice. Therefore, the angels who, with awe, attend this sacrifice attend each Mass with you.

Simultaneously, you are present to them in the moment of the Gloria as they announce the Savior in Bethlehem. The thought is enough to bend the mind of any genius. Nevertheless, by singing with active participation and awareness in the Mass and drawing others to do so, this is indeed the reality in which you participate. In fact, the joining of your music with the angels' becomes even more significant as the drama of the Mass unfolds.

For now, however, please remember how at Christmas, with all the sparkle and trappings of the day surrounding you, moved with joy, you probably sing *Gloria in excelsis Deo* with all your heart. May we do so always in the Gloria. We are not reminding the congregation of a past story about the birth of the baby Jesus. With the angels, we are announcing His imminent arrival in the Mass.[54]

Whereas the priest acts in the very person of Christ in the Mass (not only as an *alter Christus*, another Christ, as you and I might aspire to become, but as *ipse Christus*, Christ Himself), I wonder if we might reasonably recognize that beginning at the Gloria, the choir, in a completely and ontologically different way, is united to the choirs of angels—acting in their place on Earth—when it announces these sacred realities. Of course, your choir is not united to the angels in person and transformed as the priest is to Christ, but it is unarguably united to them in purpose. *You* assist the *angels* in their mission!

Are the angels truly present at Mass? Does your music truly mingle with theirs? Lest you think this is merely the pious theory

---

[54] The Gloria, and our joyful response to God's mercy, however, doesn't end at Christmas but only begins. In fact, with its every word taken from Scripture, it tells the history of salvation. This is wonderfully and completely explained in Dr. Edward Sri's book *A Biblical Walk through the Mass*. It, along with Christopher Carstens's *A Devotional Journey into the Mass*, is essential reading for the parish musician who wants to understand the scriptural basis for every word they pray in song. Rather than attempt to replicate Dr. Sri's extensive work regarding the whole text of the Gloria, I encourage you to read it.

of an enthusiastic music lover, consider what the saints say. Saint Augustine tells us that "the angels surround and help the priest when he is celebrating Mass." Saint Gregory the Great explains that "the heavens open and multitudes of angels come to assist in the holy sacrifice."

Jean Cardinal Danielou, in *The Angels and Their Mission*, assembles the observations of the Church Fathers as early as the fourth century and the teachings of the Church that reveal to us this truth.

> "The angels surround the priest," writes St. John Chrysostom. "The whole sanctuary and the space before the altar is filled with the heavenly Powers come to honor Him who is present upon the altar." And elsewhere: "Think now of what kind of choir you are going to enter. Although vested with a body, you have been judged worthy to join the Powers of heaven in singing the praises of Him who is Lord of all."[55]

What happens at Mass, then, is indeed what has traditionally been depicted. The angels assist the priest, and the choir assists the angels! (That ordering of things alone should give us pause to consider Who the priest is in the context of the Mass!)

Beginning with the Gloria, this relationship of heavenly realities is singularly important for the musician to understand. It will become increasingly more so as the Mass progresses. If our eyes could see beyond the dimensions to which they are limited, what we would witness is this:

---

[55] Jean Danielou, *The Angels and Their Mission* (Manchester, New Hampshire: Sophia Institute Press, 2009), 68.

Plate No. 13 from *Catechisme en Images,*
Maison De La Bonne Presse, 1908.

When I show such a picture to my first communicants, they often have the same question that many of us may have. Why is so much of it hidden? If the angels are descending, and the altar is Calvary, and Jesus Himself becomes really present — if God is going to do all those amazing things — why are they hidden from us? Everybody would believe if they could just see what the Mass really is!

Their observation, however, is also their answer and ours. If God fully revealed the intersection of Heaven and Earth, time and eternity that is the Mass, more than He already does in the miracles He gives us, everybody would indeed believe. However, we would believe not because our hearts sought Him, but because He made His presence and power so unavoidably obvious.

This is how it will be for us once we die and see Jesus at our judgment. It's the reason that seeking a relationship with Him now contains a different possibility than it will once we've seen Him plainly. If what takes place in the Mass was fully revealed by God to our senses, we would believe in God as we believe in the fundamental forces of nature — not out of a loving faith that seeks Him but out of a practical fear of a proven power so vast.

God gave us free will and always gives us a choice in desiring a relationship with Him or not. A gentleman wouldn't ask a lady out on a date while brandishing some display of overwhelming power, such as waving a machine gun. Why? Because he could never know, nor could she, whether she said yes out of love or out of fear. Her free will would be violated, and in that, her love could never be true.

So how does God extend the question to us? In many ways, and especially in the Mass, He uses beauty. He uses artists like you! You, with the angels, are the "wingman" in His proposal of intimacy to humanity, much as Gabriel was God's wingman in seeking Mary's *fiat*.[56]

Here lies another reason why the fate of souls depends on the beauty and sincerity of your music: the angels need your hands and voices to do their work on Earth, where human ears can hear.[57]

---

[56] I must in fairness attribute this angel pun, which I love, to my mother, who has a special devotion to Archangel Gabriel and thus special insight.

[57] They do not "need," of course, in the sense they could not accomplish things better themselves but because God desires that we choose and strive to play a part, and your part is critical! Imagine

Again, please allow the dignity and importance of your work as a parish musician to penetrate your heart. Let us who make music implore the help of the angels that we may assist them well!

Reminders for the Gloria

- In stark contrast to the Kyrie, the Gloria expresses intense and joyful gratitude to God for His mercy by proclaiming His glory!
- You join with the very angels themselves in their song of praise. You sing with them the words they proclaimed to the shepherds at Bethlehem and help your congregation, like the shepherds, to realize that Christ will be incarnate among them!
- Ask yourself if your music communicates these feelings, and if it does not, choose a selection that does. Consider an upbeat tempo, a major key, and lush instrumentation. Avoid using exactly the same choices with which you delivered the Kyrie.
- You probably sing these words at Christmas with great meaning and joy. You should feel and communicate those sentiments no less at each and every Mass!

---

how much better the party after a sports victory is for team members who played in the game than for those who sat on the bench. By not "winning" all by Himself, as He could have done, God allows us the opportunity to participate in His plan of salvation. We get our time on the field when we work hard at things such as making the best music possible for the Mass.

Music and Meaning in the Mass

Liturgy of the Word

Having come through this initial drama of entering inward, repenting of our sins and imploring God's mercy, and giving joyful thanks for receiving it, we begin a distinctly new phase. In this part of the Mass, we journey toward the second peak on the mystic's map, where we begin to know God better. This phase is essential in our growth toward intimacy, and you, as a musician, require a special understanding as to why.

I'm powerfully reminded of a beautiful movie called *A Walk in the Clouds*. It begins with a soldier's mistake. While at war, he pours out his heart in daily letters to his sweetheart. He reveals his past life, his present love, and his hopes for their future together—all in very specific detail. When he returns home, and runs to her arms, he expects to find a person who knows him well.

It turns out, however, that she wasn't much of a reader. She kept the letters as nice souvenirs, all in order in a suitcase, but mostly unopened. She figured she had the gist. This is very often what we do with God's Word. Obviously, the soldier's relationship with his sweetheart couldn't work, especially when a very different woman read the letters and came to love the man she got to know there.

Similarly, we can't begin to hope for true closeness with God, either in the spiritual life or the Mass, if we are like the girlfriend who wasn't too interested in reading the love letters. If we progress to the second peak in the drama through which your music ushers souls, God is giving us the chance to grow in our understanding of who He is. He hopes that, like the girlfriend who ultimately won the hero in the movie, we might fall in love with the person we get to know.

Your job as a musician, like a troubadour hired to play at a dinner by a man who intends to propose to his love, is to facilitate this romance. In this section of the Mass, you have the opportunity to announce and present God's love letters to humanity in song. We all know how much more movingly our sentiments to another can be expressed when set to music, and God charges you with the awesome responsibility of making His words heard and felt.

Music and Meaning in the Mass

The Responsorial Psalm

If you are given the opportunity to sing the psalm, you are praying in the very same way that Jesus Himself prayed at the first Mass. He led His friends in singing the psalms, and the fact that He did this models for us the importance of music's place in liturgy. Matthew (26:30) and Mark (14:26) tell us that the Last Supper ended only "after singing."

Psalms are poems meant for singing. In fact, because of the way that God's Word in the psalms formed such a central part of Jesus' culture, prayer and song were more closely bonded than they are for us now. This is an incredible loss for us!

The musical tradition of these prayers was so beloved by the Jewish people that all the psalms were attributed to King David, their warrior-poet-hero, who conquered as effectively with the harp as with the sword (or slingshot). Singing the psalms allowed God's Word to permeate their daily lives. When you hear a song repeatedly, do you not have this same experience? We even teach our children the alphabet this way!

It's a shame today that we don't take the kind of time necessary to let the psalms pervade our lives. It's typically only priests and religious who pray the Liturgy of the Hours,[58] which involves reading assigned psalms every day, so that it becomes a familiar rhythm, as it was for Jesus and the Jews of His time. For instance,

---

[58] There's no reason it should just be priests and religious who pray the Liturgy of the Hours, by the way. You can try yourself—even just by praying Lauds in the morning or Vespers in the evening. It's easier than ever today because you can access the text immediately on cell phone apps rather than struggle to master the breviary with its pretty-colored but complicated ribbons. Engaging with God's music in the psalms is a wonderful way to grow spiritually as a musician and to bring your prayer life more deeply to the Mass.

I recently texted a friar friend who was leaving on a long trip, "Don't forget to write!"

His immediate comeback: "If I forget you, O Jerusalem, let my right hand wither!"[59] Why did he have such an unexpected, poetic response at his fingertips? Because when people pray the psalms regularly, God's Word pervades their minds with its beauty and remains present, always ready to associate their thoughts with a holy sentiment.

That's how Jesus was! He prayed and sang with us in this very way! How do we know? Not only at the Last Supper but even in His final moments on the Cross, the psalms still wove in and out of His thoughts, His prayers, and His conversation, at the hour of His death as much as they had in life.

At the Last Supper, He would have sung Psalms 114–118, the thanksgiving songs concluding the Passover meal. Considering that He was leaving to go to the Garden of Gethsemane, imagine how His song must have pervaded the content of His prayer when it contained words like this:

> I was caught by the cords of death,
> The snares of Sheol had seized me;
> I felt agony and dread.
> Then I called on the name of the LORD,
> O LORD, save my life! (Psalm 116:3–4)

When a person is in his greatest physical distress, we might say we have a certain insight into the way his mind truly works, as he is unable to keep up any kind of pretense. How does Jesus pray in

---

[59] This is from Psalm 137, and it is even in itself an example of the importance of music. The psalmist swears to remember Jerusalem by the use of his tongue and his right hand—the two things a poet musician needs most!

those stripped-bare moments? Even "My God, my God, why have you forsaken me?" is the beginning of Psalm 22, perfectly associated with His feelings, thoughts, and prayers at that moment.

We know then that for Jesus, our model, an intimate knowledge of God's Word ran like a soundtrack through His mind and His life. We know that the psalms formed many running themes of that musical score. What does all this mean for parish musicians tasked with leading the responsorial psalm?

Today, unfortunately, the responsorial psalm might be the only exposure many people get to the psalms during the week. This is not unlike how stained-glass windows in medieval cathedrals might have been the only Gospel many people of the time could "read." Again, the role and influence of beauty is striking, especially the way in which you, tasked with producing artistic beauty in the Mass, are associated with the angels in bringing God's proposal to humanity.

If your congregation is going to be illuminated by God's Word in this phase of the Mass, and moved by some of the first and most beautiful letters He wrote to His people, it becomes your task both to present the psalm clearly and completely and to help root the psalm firmly in their consciousness. Fortunately, as always, there's multivalent wisdom in the Church's solution. It's a *responsorial* psalm.

How do you imagine that even the Child Jesus learned the very first psalms that underscored His prayer life — even before He was old enough to read and study Scripture? The psalms pervaded Mary and Joseph's daily rhythm, and Jesus most certainly heard them sung at home. How do we teach our own children a song? We sing a portion, and they sing it back!

It's no coincidence that the responsorial psalm also has this call-and-response design. The response portion typically summarizes or embodies the main feeling or idea of the psalm. It has a unique melodic setting, whereas the remainder is more simply "read" in song. The response, if you will, is the takeaway "sound bite" from each psalm.[60]

Ideally, then, this sound bite should function as something of an earworm. An earworm is a brief melody that, even unbidden, insinuates itself repetitively in our thoughts. Think of the Meow Mix jingle, and you will know what I mean. A day or an hour from now, you will curse me for calling it to mind when you find yourself humming it unintentionally.

I'm not recommending we use melodies as trivial as those that predominate in advertising, of course, nor am I saying that the psalm response should resemble the rhythmically-dominated pop refrains that haunt us today. They should, however, help us to remember the heart of the psalm as easily as we remember that "the best part of waking up is Folgers in your cup." Musically, what can we do to work toward accomplishing this? Perhaps we need some new psalm settings with this goal in mind.

If you are working from existing settings, however, simply remembering that your goal is to teach through beauty, just as Mary and Joseph did, will go far toward accomplishing it. Because of the variability of the psalm texts, no musical moods can be usefully prescribed, and because we do not sing in the language the psalms were written, we can't enjoy their rhythm the way that the people of Jesus' time would have. That leaves us only the option of declaiming clearly in the body of the psalm without excessive or distracting musical interference and using all the musical tools in

---

[60] There are one or two of these that are incredibly memorable to me. "If today you hear his voice, harden not your hearts," for instance. Or "*Oh Dios, crea en mí un corazon puro.*" Think of psalm responses that do the same for you and ask yourself why they remain with you.

our arsenal to make the response memorably beautiful and compel-
lingly singable for the congregation.

Reminders for the Responsorial Psalm

- You are singing here to imprint God's Word on the hearts
  of your congregation, using a "teaching" method of call
  and response.
- It is essential that the response be repeatable, singable,
  and memorable. Choose a melodic "earworm" if at all
  possible, as you want it to crop up in your congregation's
  thoughts later in the day and the week.
- As the psalms differ so greatly, no recommendation for
  considerations like tempo, key, or mood can be applicable to all. However, ensure that your choices reflect the
  sentiment of the text. Avoid dirge-like tempi for joyful
  proclamations, for instance.
- Because this is the Liturgy of the Word, and because the
  text is variable, and therefore less familiar than other parts
  of the Mass, it is especially important that the congregation hear and absorb the text. Enunciate and sing slowly
  enough to be understood.

The Mystic Design of Music in the Mass

The Alleluia (Gospel Acclamation)

The next task for the choir along the second peak of the Mass is the Alleluia (or Gospel Acclamation appropriate to the liturgical season). I must return to my *A Walk in the Clouds* analogy to mention that it fails in one respect. Though the soldier might have "poured himself into" his letters, the letters weren't he. The Word of God, however, is, in fact, the Word—the second Person of the Trinity, who is Jesus Himself (John 1:1).

Jesus is not physically present in His Body in the Word, as He is uniquely present in the Eucharist, but the Word is still He. Sometimes when I can't sleep because God feels distant, I hug the nearest Bible, because He's there—present for me and for all of us. (It's a childish gesture, I know, but it acknowledges a simple truth.) So, if the job of the parish musician is to increase reverence for Jesus' presence in the Mass, pointing to the reality of His presence as the Word is our principle aim in this phase of the unfolding drama.

In each reading of the Liturgy of the Word, more and more of Christ is revealed. The Alleluia announces a new height in this revelation. The Alleluia requires musical intensification, because the Gospel is the Word of God spoken to us from the very lips of the Word of God incarnate. This brain twister is worth wrapping our minds around, as it can influence profoundly how we sing the Alleluia. When we read the Gospel, Jesus, present, addresses us directly.

It's interesting that standing to attention accompanies this music, as thinking of the circumstance though a military lens might help our music expressively. In many militaries, if an officer who outranks you should enter the room, the appropriate response would be to stand and salute. If the king commanding the army were to enter the room to address his troops, he'd be greeted by this formality and, in addition, a musical fanfare.

Music and Meaning in the Mass

The Alleluia is that fanfare. Alleluia means "Praise the Lord!' It is akin in this context to shouting, "Hooray for the King!"

What considerations make for an appropriate fanfare? Musical moods to consider should imply nobility, and, for a King so beloved as ours, sentiments of exultation and joy! A major key, a rhythm and tempo that convey dignity, and full-bodied instrumentation will probably serve best for the scene you accompany.[61]

Gospel acclamations outside Ordinary Time, while hailing the King with His people's praise, reflect the sentiment appropriate for the liturgical season. This could be slightly more reserved in instrumentation and perhaps could even admit a minor key or less overtly joyful mode if it were to invoke a quieter awe for Advent or penitent hope in Lent. The Christmas and Easter seasons call for an increase in the acclamation's joyful exuberance — even if that means the music is slightly less stately than in Ordinary Time.

Again, and in all cases, as long as your musical choices pass the suggested test — meaning that they could meaningfully fit the scene you are accompanying (which is, in the Gospel Acclamation, the entrance of a king) — you can be certain that you are making the right choices. Perhaps you have an exceptional Gospel Acclamation in mind that goes against the general suggestions here. For instance, it might be minor in Ordinary Time in order to maintain dramatic continuity within a particular Mass setting.

---

[61] My Tolkienesque imagination is reminded, both here and later in the Sanctus, of *The Return of the King*. Let your mind be flooded too with whatever beautiful art represents the salvific drama of this moment to you, as these thoughts will fuel your prayerful expression of the music with emotional meaning and guide your choices appropriately. If your Alleluia wouldn't sound right welcoming Aragorn to Gondor (a made-up story), it certainly wouldn't be right for welcoming Christ to the altar (a critical reality).

If it genuinely fits the scene, it's a good choice. If it does not, don't let any other factor influence your decision. I take the time to call to mind the test again now, because as this section of the Mass ends and we progress toward the next peak on the mystic's map, the one in which unfathomable intimacy is approached, the importance of fitting the scene becomes increasingly more crucial.

Reminders for the Alleluia

- The Alleluia can be compared to the fanfare for a king.
- If "Hail to the Chief" announces an earthly president, what must the Alleluia sound like to announce the Word Himself, present in the Gospel reading?
- You are calling those around you to come to attention and welcome Him, so the Alleluia must both seize their attention and encourage their exultation.
- Consider a major key, a rhythm and tempo that convey dignity, and full-bodied instrumentation.

Music and Meaning in the Mass

Liturgy of the Eucharist

Though I've limited my discussion of the unfolding of the Mass exclusively to its musical moments, it's worth noting that the transition from the Liturgy of the Word to the Liturgy of the Eucharist, or the second peak on the mystic's map to the third, cloud-piercing peak of intimacy with God, takes place only after the typically spoken Creed. (However, what follows might incite you to make this critical moment musical once again by revisiting the tradition of the Creed as a participatory chant for the congregation. It would not be more difficult than the usual setting of the Our Father sometimes chanted by American congregations.)

The time of getting to know God in His Word approaches its summit on the map of the Mass with a powerful and complete profession of faith by the individual soul. In the Creed, each congregant says, "I believe." Though it's possible to remain in one's pew after this point and go through the motions that follow, it's not truly possible to go further, in active participation, without having made that affirmation from one's very depths.

During the Roman persecution of the Church, the division in the Mass marked by the Creed labeled what came before it the Liturgy of the Catechumens and what came after it the Liturgy of the Faithful. A deep valley existed there[62] and a profound decision for the soul who desired intimacy with Jesus in the Eucharist. Unlike today, those who couldn't yet fully profess couldn't remain present for what happened next.

They left at that point, to continue with their preparation toward initiation and to consider the choice they would make. To assent fully, to declare "I believe," meant to label oneself a Christian and a target for grave violence because of that decision. The

---

[62] This bears strong parallels to the deep valley that separates the second and third peaks in the spiritual life.

catechumens had to ask themselves, "Am I willing to offer myself completely to God, that I may accept His complete offering of Himself to me?"

Put another way, "Am I willing to abandon everything to gain Him who is everything?" In the spiritual life, only a complete yes to this question, in which a soul actually desires and allows God to strip it of all that is less than desire for Him, results in progress toward the unitive stage. However, a reflection of this opportunity to say yes, and to receive Our Lord with a desire that is only for Him, exists for us in the Mass too.

As my little student's love of the modern martyrs her age reminded me, the grave danger of this decision still exists, as a yes to this question can mean death. In fact, it does now for even more of our brothers and sisters than those who suffered under Roman persecution. People die today at numbers that approach the modern definition of genocide.[63] Their yes is a true self-offering.

Does our continuation in the Mass from this point on mean the same thing? Do we somehow gloss over it without active participation, without recognizing it, and without taking part in it? Does our music help those who continue forward in the Mass with us to understand or be moved by these truths?

---

[63] "Christian Persecution 'at Near Genocide Levels,'" BBC News, May 3, 2019, https://www.bbc.com/news/uk-48146305.

Music and Meaning in the Mass

The Offertory

In the Offertory, our music must invite the souls in the pews to make the offering of self to which they are called. I bring up all of the above because it's easy to think that the job of the parish musician at this moment is to provide some musical "cover," lest people become bored, while Father is busy preparing the altar and the ushers take up the collection. Very rarely does the song associate those two actions with each other.

However, they're closely related, and it's here that the souls in the pews have a particularly active part to play besides fumbling through purses and wallets. Yes, they should put some money in the collection basket if they can afford to do so because the parish needs to keep the heat on, the poor need to be fed, and so forth. However, the purpose of what happens here isn't primarily financial, and even those who can't afford to give money still may make the most valuable contribution of all.

It's here that, in our hearts, we are invited to contribute our prayers and labors, joys and sufferings, gifts and struggles — in fact, everything that we have, do, and are — as offerings to be presented on the altar, where they form some little contribution to Christ's great offering. With the gifts that are brought up to the altar, the act of adding something such as money (a product of our labor) is supposed to remind us of this, not distract us from doing it. The song we choose here can be of great help.

Ideally, the song should take up the theme of offering or of responding generously to God's invitation, perhaps as it was presented in some unique way in the readings of the day. Musical considerations are much less limited here than at many other points in the Mass with regard to key, rhythm, instrumentation, and so forth. The things that are important at this point are those covered primarily in chapter 4. In every way you can, simply ensure that this song is beautiful.

If an example is helpful in knowing what to search for, I think of "Lord, When You Came to the Seashore." It has themes of Jesus' seeking not one's riches but one's heart in consent, one's hands in His labor. Musically, few melodies could be said to be as memorably beautiful. It is properly ordered in terms of the precedence of melody over harmony and harmony over rhythm. Finally, it fittingly accompanies the "scene" of what is transpiring spiritually.[64]

Reminders for the Offertory

- The Offertory is not a moment of musical cover. It must inspire a spiritual action critical to the Mass. Here, all souls are invited to offer something of themselves upon the altar, to be united with Christ's sacrifice.
- Your music can help lead them toward the offering of their *whole* selves—becoming saints—but they must feel that this is, in fact, what is occurring in the Mass.
- While the song text should relate to this self-offering, the mood, key, tempo, and every other specific musical consideration for this moment may vary.
- This is a moment when congregational singing is not essential. Therefore, you have increased freedom with regard to instrumentation and may perhaps even choose to feature some higher levels of technical proficiency to create inspiring beauty!

---

[64] Others that come to mind for similar reasons are "Here I Am Lord," "To You, O God, I Lift My Soul," "Unless a Grain of Wheat," "All That We Have and All that We Offer," and "Where Your Treasure Is."

Music and Meaning in the Mass

The Sanctus (Eucharistic Acclamations)

With the consent and self-offering in the Creed and the Offertory, the Mass formally and fully enters into the Liturgy of the Eucharist — the third and greatest peak and the destination of the mystic journey. Very fittingly, the first thing sung now is the Sanctus. This is a thrice-repeated declaration, as we found earlier in the Kyrie.

Thrice-repeated prayers are not the products of stumped or stuttering lyricists but are critical signals that intently try to communicate to us. In ancient Hebrew, the ultimate superlative was a three-time repetition. This still resonates today.

Have you ever been at a campsite and been the first to see an approaching bear? You might first simply point and, taken with fear, with quivering breath say, "Bear." Then, more firmly, trying to rouse your friends to action, manage to say, "Bear!" Then, as a fuller realization begins to grip you, "BEAR!"

Now, instead of something reasonably powerful, like a bear, what if you were trying to alert others to the approach of something omnipotent? What if their reaction to it wouldn't save only their earthly lives but also their eternal ones? How desperately would you *need* to express to them what approaches?

Love, of course, not fear, is our end, but fear is certainly a wise place to begin. Proverbs tells us "the beginning of wisdom is fear of the LORD" (9:10). Complementarily, the First Letter of John tells us that "perfect love drives out fear" (4:18).

In a step beyond mere fear, the otherwise inexpressibly superlative aspect of the repetition can speak to us as well. We're not just trying to say that what is happening and Who is approaching is really holy. We're saying "Holy. Holy. Holy."

There is nothing else that could be said. Quite literally, the angels themselves can't express it better. Repeatedly in Scripture, when both Isaiah and John are given a glimpse of Heaven, they reveal to us that this is the chant of the Seraphim (Isaiah 6:3; Revelation 4:8).

These passages should draw our reflection as musicians in the Mass to understand better the heavenly dimension of the liturgy, in which we participate with the angels, and how seriously close to God we begin to approach. I offer one for meditation below, in which we can see a prefigurement of all that may take place for the soul in the spiritual life and the Mass, except the Eucharistic union. That, even the great prophet who saw Heaven itself could not enjoy, and yet we can.

> I saw the Lord seated on a high and lofty throne, with the train of his garment filling the temple. Seraphim were stationed above; each of them had six wings: with two they covered their faces, with two they covered their feet, and with two they hovered. One cried out to the other:
> "Holy, holy, holy is the LORD of hosts!
> All the earth is filled with his glory!"
> At the sound of that cry, the frame of the door shook and the house was filled with smoke.
> Then I said, "Woe is me, I am doomed! For I am a man of unclean lips, living among a people of unclean lips, and my eyes have seen the King, the LORD of hosts!" Then one of the seraphim flew to me, holding an ember which he had taken with tongs from the altar.
> He touched my mouth with it. "See," he said, "now that this has touched your lips, your wickedness is removed, your sin purged."
> Then I heard the voice of the Lord saying, "Whom shall I send? Who will go for us?" "Here I am," I said; "send me!" (Isaiah 6:1–8)

Music and Meaning in the Mass

In *The Angels and Their Mission*, Jean Cardinal Daniélou explains the moment of the Sanctus with utter clarity. He states:

> This chant of the Seraphim expresses holy fear. It describes the awe felt by even the highest creatures in the presence of the infinite divine excellence. And this enables us to understand better the holiness of the Eucharist, which leads us, with the Seraphim, into the presence of the all-holy God, hidden only by the fragile species of bread and wine.[65]

Here, our prayer is united with the angels, not at Bethlehem, but in eternal glory. What music could possibly express any of this? If you are not overwhelmed by the question and stumped, perhaps you are not yet processing it fully. How can our music convey the same truth as it is the purpose of the host of Heaven to declare and do it so that souls are led to recognize it?

If the question does cause you anxiety, and it is of the sort that propels you to give nothing but your ever-improving best, then I think this appropriate and good. If the question gives you anxiety of the type that may tempt you to despair, however, I have a thought that might help. I myself experience both kinds of anxiety, and this thought both motivates and comforts me.

If something that can be called music exists in Heaven, and it seems very reasonable that it does, that music must be free of every imperfection. I imagine that it must, for instance, lack dissonance. However, for us on Earth, such things give music meaning. Harmony wouldn't exist effectively for us without dissonance because of the tension and resulting draw toward resolution it generates. We could not "feel" resolution without tension.

This dynamic creates our emotional involvement with music. Its sensed drama affects us deeply, because it mimics a longing

---

[65] Danielou, *The Angels and Their Mission*, 71.

that is characteristic of the experience of every human being. We can respond to it with many things, but it never fully ceases here, since it is the magnetic pull of the soul's internal compass toward God. The soul knows it's not where it belongs until its essential straining comes to rest.[66]

In this imperfection, this intrinsic "unfinishedness," even our most joyful music always contains within it the expression of our capacity for suffering. Now, it is often said that the angels, if they were capable of envy, would envy humanity for two things: our ability to receive the Eucharist, that we may experience that particular great intimacy with Jesus, and our capacity to suffer, that we may offer ourselves to help Him to bear His pain. This would mean, quite astoundingly if it is true, that our music is capable of communicating something that the music of the angels is not.

One might even go so far as to imagine Christ on His throne, hearing the perfection of angel choirs, but having within His human experience the longing, straining, weeping, gorgeousness of the Jewish folk music and psalm settings of His time. Moved with nostalgia, would He ever say, "Come on, Seraphic friends, won't you sing my Mom's old favorite just once for me?" If He did this, it seems that the angels couldn't do what a living human can do now.

Your choir's difference from the heavenly chorus is a critical one. It is the reason that it is with your hands and voices that earthly praise of the Mass must be offered. You, and you alone, can express and inspire longing in a way that Heaven cannot, and it is perhaps most essentially *our longing itself* that best consoles Our

---

[66] Saint Augustine famously put it, "My soul is restless, O Lord, until it rests in thee." Saint John of the Cross aptly likened it to the force of gravity, continually drawing us to the center of mass, but only as closely as whatever blocks us allows.

Lord and disposes us here to intimacy with Him in the spiritual life and in the Eucharist.[67]

As it unfolds, the Sanctus unites the worship of Heaven and Earth. In Jesus' life, when was He most fully and widely recognized as Messiah and King? It was during His entry into Jerusalem when, throwing down their cloaks and cutting palm branches, people celebrated before Him in the best recognition of His true identity of which they were capable. The words of the Sanctus contain the psalm the people would have sung as they did so, Psalm 118.

In this one moment of music, the Mass unites us through time and eternity to both scenes—the one in Heaven and the one in Jerusalem—in which, if drawn into active sung prayer themselves, our congregation participates with their own worship. Musical moods that might be appropriate must include utter reverence, ideally moving from awe to longing and ultimately resolving toward triumphant acclamation. Any key or mode that can accomplish these highly specific goals is appropriate. Instrumentation may be at its most powerful, and rhythm cannot distract or predominate.

We see now that while the Sanctus may commence with fear, it does not resolve there. In the Sanctus, our longing must tran-scend our fear. Really, this parallels our experience of love to the degree that it is reflected in all relationships, but the Sanctus is our response to Love par excellence. However, if the emotional and musical experience of the Sanctus doesn't begin in fear, then we are simply asleep to the realities taking place.[68]

---

[67] With reference to this point in the spiritual life, Saint John of the Cross says, "The desire for God is the preparation for union with Him."

[68] We cannot long for what we don't first recognize and then come to know, in this case, at least well enough to be awed by. These things were accomplished in the purgative and illuminative phases of the Mass, which now, at the Sanctus, we both sustain and transcend!

The Mystic Design of Music in the Mass

My emphasis on fear is a wake-up call. My emphasis on longing is the loving response to which artists can uniquely respond and lead. This, the Sanctus, is the moment in which music can perhaps most powerfully and effectively lead humanity in its response to God. It is here that the soul will be its best disposed to receive Him in the Eucharistic union that will come next.

If we think it is possible to do this with anything less than our best effort, and without our full understanding and the employment of the best musical tools at our disposal, combined with our constant striving at their mastery at whatever level we are capable, then we most certainly will fail. This, tragically, is what is already happening. And this, my friends, in the same way that a freshly equipped cavalry can turn the tide of battle, is something we musicians, together with the help of the angels and the sheer grace of God, can combat.

Reminders for the Sanctus

- Thrice-repeated prayers communicate a superlative meaning. You sing, "Holy, *Holy*, HOLY," to express that He who approaches is unfathomably so. Your sung adoration joins with that of the highest orders of angels, as they are present and worship at the same Mass you attend, in awe of Christ's sacrifice on the altar.
- At this point, you are upon the great heights of the mystical realities of the Mass, and your music must lead those present to express their love in recognition of Christ. Ask yourself if your musical setting and performance of the Sanctus fittingly accompanies the scene unfolding, and strive to ensure that it does.
- However, no music we are capable of producing on Earth can adequately express this worship. Nevertheless, in

God's plan, you are called upon to do what the angels cannot — to make its truth accessible to human ears and, with Heaven and Earth, express to God the cry of our human longing.

- Beyond any specific musical recommendations, that realization should awaken in you a relentless quest for artistic excellence and devoted reliance on the assistance of the angels. It is said that the angels perfect our prayers. While you help them to do what they cannot, they will help you to do what you cannot, for the sake of the souls you lead in this song.

The Mystic Design of Music in the Mass

The Great Amen

This is the first piece of music that is sung after the words of con-secration, with Jesus present on the altar, the sacrifice of Calvary underway. Call to mind the suggestion that even the angels long to offer suffering with Jesus on Calvary—a privilege He extends, however, only to us. In Colossians 1:24, Saint Paul tells us:

> Now I rejoice in my sufferings for your sake, and in my flesh
> I am filling up what is lacking in the afflictions of Christ on
> behalf of his body, which is the Church.

Christ's sacrifice is perfect and eternal, of course, so what lacks in His afflictions is not anything that Christ hasn't already offered, but rather our acceptance of and participation in His gift.[69] Nothing is lacking in a perfectly planned party, for instance — the host might have gone to every expense to extend each invitation, prepare each delicacy, and offer each gift — but at the same time, *something* is lacking if the guest for whom it was all prepared never arrives. In the Great Amen, we have an unparalleled chance to respond like the guest who accepts the invitation and brings some tiny gift of gratitude of his or her own — perhaps a bottle of wine so that the host has to pour out just a little less of his.

My mom is a wonderful party guest. She always arrives not just with a token for the host but with gifts that show forth her abundance of generosity! When she piles the platters of goodies she

---

[69] This is perhaps best explained in Pope Saint John Paul II's Apos-tolic Letter *Salvifici Doloris* (February 11, 1984). In more personal and devotional terms, a wonderful guide to this understanding is Father Michael Gaitley's *Consoling the Heart of Jesus: A Do-It-Yourself Retreat Inspired by the Spiritual Exercises of St. Ignatius* (Stockbridge, MA: Marian Helpers Center, 2010). It's a book I recommend to everyone, but especially musicians who seek to enter into this most powerful mystery.

has labored over into the arms of the host, what kind of friendship does it imply that they share?

My mom is so counted on, in fact, that an overwhelmed party host might confide in her a few days early that he could really use some help with a particular course. Instead of offering just a token gift, then, my mom takes on some of the labor. The invitation to participate with Christ on the altar is similar, and our response can be as stingy as one who accepts the invitation and brings nothing or as generous as my mother's.

Our gift, whatever its size, is always unutterably miniscule compared with the sacrifice of Christ, which is already complete without our offering. However, especially considering the tender Heart of Jesus, it's hard to imagine that He would reject even a broken flower offered to Him in love by a tiny child by saying, "Humph! I created all the flowers of the world, and that one was already mine. Take your silly little gift and go home!" No, our little offerings mean much more to Jesus than we can understand.

Otherwise, how can we imagine God saying what He does in Isaiah 63:5? Saint Thérèse was especially moved by meditating on this passage in the context of Christ's Passion, and she resolved never to allow Him to say the same because of her.[70] It reads:

> I looked about, but there was no one to help,
> I was appalled that there was no one to lend support;
> So my own arm brought me victory.

Readings such as this imply that Jesus longs to be helped, but how can our sufferings help Him? Saint Paul gives us more insight. Speaking of the body in 1 Corinthians 12:26–27, he says:

---

[70] Letter to Céline, July 18, 1890.

If one part suffers, all the parts suffer with it; if one part is honored, all the parts share its joy. Now you are Christ's body, and individually parts of it.

Christ is the head of His Mystical Body, the Church. A body, as Saint Paul tells us and our experience affirms, suffers and enjoys everything together. No one has ever jammed a toe and remarked in the moment, "Boy, I'm feeling great! Tough luck for my suffering toe." Similarly, a cool washcloth on the head can comfort a fever affecting the whole body.

Jesus doesn't presume simply to appropriate our sufferings or joys, however. As always, He seeks our consent. He accepts from us only what is freely offered, so if we are moved to help Him, as St. Thérèse was, we must remember to offer!

While in the spiritual life we may hope to always do as Saint Paul models, nowhere do we have the opportunity to make that offering as perfectly as in our participation in the Great Amen of the Mass. Recall that the Offertory song encouraged us not to present only our pocket change but our more valuable assets—our sufferings, our joys, our lives, and our very selves—as gifts upon the altar. They were gifts for sacrifice.

At this point in the Mass, the priest lifts up Jesus[71] and says the prayer that begins, "Through Him, with Him, and in Him." We have one word to sing in response: Amen. Its meaning encompasses so much. Yes. I affirm. I consent. So may it be. Like Mary, we give our *fiat* (Luke 1:38).

When we sing here, our prayer is "Yes, I assent that I offer everything through, with, and in Jesus, in the unity of the Holy

---

[71] John 12:32 gives me chills in this context: "When I am lifted up from the earth, I will draw everyone to myself." In the Mass, we see layers of biblical truth too deep to comprehend in a lifetime!

Spirit, to the glory of God the Father." If we sing amen to this, and mean it, it becomes, literally, humanity's Great Amen. This Amen is our part in the perfect sacrifice.

We make no response or gift at all, however, if we don't participate with awareness in this prayer. The faithful in the pews will similarly be less inclined to respond if we don't lead them. Without our acceptance, His gift is for nothing. Without our participation, He suffers needlessly alone.

Interestingly, God is never outdone in His generosity. While such participation seems like our attempt at a gift to Jesus, it can, in fact, be an even greater gift to us. It transforms and gives meaning to our lives in a fallen world.

Imagine if, in the Great Amen, every soul in every pew felt the consolation that not one moment of their lives might be wasted. In it, the daily drudgery of data entry in a dark cubicle, the thankless hassle of unseen housekeeping, life's little frustrations and failures and injustices, right along with life's great tragedies, all become the stuff of supernatural superheroes. These things console Jesus' Sacred Heart by sharing freely in His suffering and, quite literally, help Him save the world!

Musically, what can we do to lead the Great Amen with all of this intent? First, and most powerfully, we must understand it and long to express it ourselves. Musical moods to consider should communicate the ultimate importance of this Amen and can shade it with either gravity or triumph. Anything light or trivial with regard to rhythm or melody should be avoided.

No practice or effort should be spared in ensuring the technical quality and beauty of the Great Amen musically, as it and the Sanctus form the two most critical musical expressions of the Mass. The Great Amen should never give the impression of an afterthought, as we might admit today that it often does.[72] Instead, it should be a moment that resonates in the hearts of all who hear and join in it, consoling them through the unfolding of their lives. In short, let's make the Great Amen great!

Reminders for the Great Amen

- This moment can culminate a soul's self-offering participation in the mystic journey of the Mass, uniting it with Christ's sacrifice on the altar, lifting from Him a burden of suffering and consoling Him in profound intimacy.
- Or, it might not. If our music makes this moment feel like an afterthought or an arbitrary interlude rather than the height of the congregation's active, participatory prayer, the chance can be lost.
- Knowing *why* you sing the Great Amen will make all the difference in *how* you sing it.
- The music should communicate the grave and glorious importance of this response. Anything light or trivial should be avoided, and instrumentation can be at its fullest.
- Consider everything at your disposal to encourage the congregation to experience the Great Amen as the pinnacle of their sung prayer, with its complete focus on Christ, elevated in the hands of the priest.

---

[72] Father Mike Schmitz makes the comical and tragic observation that people must not know the meaning of the prayer, because while saying Mass, he usually hears "the lame amen" instead of the Great Amen. Let's not have that happen in parishes where we lead the song!

Music and Meaning in the Mass

The Agnus Dei (Lamb of God)

Here again we find a thrice-repeated prayer, so everything previously considered with regard to the musical communication of such emphasis applies. However, this prayer contains a breathtaking difference from the others. Many of the choir's previous prayers, you might have noticed, were addressed to God the Father, or to the Father and Son jointly.

The Agnus Dei is addressed directly to the Son. Why? Because He is present Himself on the altar. In the spiritual life, we can speak to Him always in an interior way. In the Mass, particularly in the Agnus Dei, our song addresses Him in His physical presence.

Given this astounding opportunity, what do we say? The only thing that seems fitting at a moment like this is first to acknowledge His sacrifice. There is no way more biblically founded, rooted in the language of love that God Himself teaches us on our mystic journey, than to address Him as the Lamb of God.

In an earlier chapter, the question was asked how you would address someone who lay dying because he had just saved your life. I imagine running to comfort a friend who took a bullet in your stead at war, or a hero who ran in front of a bus to push you out of its path. The first thing from your lips would probably be something like this:

"You saved me! You took on yourself the horrible thing that was going to kill me! Oh, I'm so sorry, and thank you!"

Of course, you'd repeat yourself a few times. The next thought that might cross your mind is how, if this person has made such a great sacrifice for your sake, you might ever find peace. The only answer to that, if the person happens to be God, is to beg it from Him who can grant it.

Clearly, this constitutes much of what we say in the Agnus Dei:

Lamb of God, you take away the sins of the world,
    have mercy on us.
Lamb of God, you take away the sins of the world,
    have mercy on us.
Lamb of God, you take away the sins of the world,
    grant us peace.

However, why would calling Him "Lamb of God" be the most fitting way to acknowledge His sacrifice? Delving into this question will bring you into an ever-deepening understanding of Jesus' role in God's plan for salvation.[73] You will be amazed at how, from the beginning of time, God desired and put into play building blocks in human history so that He could save your soul in particular and draw it to the intimacy He desires with you in the Mass specifically.

Calling Jesus the Lamb, whose real bloodshed saves us, and whose flesh we consume, hearkens back to the earliest proofs of love that God gave to His people so that we might recognize Him in the Eucharist today and reaches forward to the eschaton (Revelation 5:6–14). Saint John the Baptist, "the greatest prophet who ever lived," according to Jesus Himself, knew God's language and the signature of His love notes better than anyone when, upon seeing Jesus, he declared to his disciples, "Behold the Lamb of God" (John 1:29). These are, of course, the very words the priest repeats when we look upon the Eucharist.

Again, in the Agnus Dei, the most important musical consideration is to know the drama you are accompanying. With that, you can hardly fail to use your music meaningfully to express it.

---

[73] I recommend doing it with the biblical scholarship of Dr. Scott Hahn, Jeff Cavins, and Dr. Edward Sri, though there is almost no serious Bible study you can do guided by the Magisterium of the Church that will not lead you to this greater understanding of the Lamb and the Mass.

Music and Meaning in the Mass

As we near the end of our examination of the Mass and its music, I pose to you the same question I asked early on, now for you to answer, hopefully, with a new arsenal of tools and understandings at your disposal. How would you sing to a person you love as he dies in order to save you? Whatever that genuine answer is, that's how the Agnus Dei must sound.

Reminders for the Agnus Dei

- Here we have the extraordinary opportunity to sing to God the Son in His physical presence.
- The most important consideration, as always, is to know the drama your music accompanies.
- In the Agnus Dei, we return to one of the first questions this book asks. How would you sing to a person you love as he sacrifices himself in order to save you? With what tender reverence? With what awe-filled respect? With what humility and gratitude?
- What would that music sound like? What would it not sound like? Your answers will provide you the best way to sing the Agnus Dei. It is your love that will lead and inspire the love of others.

The Communion Song

The parts of the Mass where you communicate a prescribed prayer essential to the congregation's active participation in the unfolding of the miraculous drama have now passed. Therefore, you have much greater freedom in your musical choices from this point forward. However, your music now has a different critical importance.

What you do now must make the best final adjustments possible to the soul's interior disposition as it approaches the altar to receive Jesus and converses with Him privately in indescribable intimacy. This is the summit of the highest peak of the mystical journey through which your music has moved souls. Here, your choices must be carefully made so as not to distract from the truth or detract from the lofty height at which you have arrived.

The song text, since you can select it on your own, should in some way reference what is occurring. It must draw people's minds toward the reality of Jesus' presence. Therefore, the song cannot be primarily about social justice or the goodness of creation or any other theme.

Even though there is a critical place for songs such as these (immediately to come), this is not it. Besides the topic of the song, the musical setting and performance must in the same way avoid "pointing" toward anything else but Jesus in the Blessed Sacrament. Techniques that cause such distraction have already been thoroughly examined.

Recall the social experiment in which a famous violinist went unrecognized in a public place. Our musical signals right now make the difference between Jesus' being recognized or not. If the Communion song doesn't sound like something that you'd sing in His presence to express your love and longing for Him, it tells people they're not in His presence, and they need not express theirs.

With regard to positive choices in mood, key, and tempo, because such a variety of song texts exists, no firm recommendations can be offered. If you do not wish to "experiment" with something so crucial, the most certain choice you can make at this point is a Eucharistic song of long-proven beauty,[74] presented with your choir's best and most attentive solemn awareness of its task, with the finest instrumentation you have available. Do this and watch hearts be opened and moved.

If you find a few Eucharistic songs that have this effect and you are able to perform them in this way, do not be afraid to repeat them frequently. If your congregation increases in familiarity with them and your practice and proficiency improve, these are all advantageous. It is better to have a few beautiful songs that point to Jesus' Real Presence than many songs, unfamiliar and less prepared, that detract from it. You can then make it a goal gradually to add songs of similar quality and impact to your repertoire.

[74] Some choices that mention the Real Presence of Christ in the Eucharist or reference John 6 include "Panis Angelicus" (Jesus our Living Bread), "Ave Verum Corpus," "O Sacrament Most Holy," "I Am the Bread of Life," "Take and Eat," "O Saving Victim," "Adoro Te Devote," and, in Spanish-speaking communities, "Alabado Sea El Santísimo Sacramento del Altar" or "Bendito, Bendito."

Reminders for the Communion Song

- At this point, your music can inspire the final adjustments to a soul's disposition of love at the point of receiving Christ in the Blessed Sacrament.
- Or, your music can distract the soul from the reality of this moment—especially if in any way it makes the Blessed Sacrament seem anything less than Who it really is.
- Your surest option is to select a theologically sound Eucharistic song of long-proven beauty that draws clear attention to Jesus' Real Presence. Unfortunately, there are far fewer available than such a critical need would demand.
- Therefore, if this means that nearly every Sunday you sing something like "Panis Angelicus" (Jesus Our Living Bread), which you perform with great technical proficiency because of constant practice, the repetition of its beauty is hardly a burden to your congregation and avoids the risk of inspiring an indifferent, unaware, or tepid reception of the Eucharist.

Music and Meaning in the Mass

The Meditation after Communion

The meditation after Communion is an even more delicate circumstance where people must be drawn inward to converse with Jesus, not outward in any other direction. Perhaps because most of us developed our capacity for sustained attention with short *Sesame Street*-style sound bites since childhood, as a society, we are already very bad at quietly maintaining focus. After we return to our pews, many of us think of the hairdo of the lady in front of us more readily than we think of the wounded Heart of the Man inside us.

Imagine how Jesus must feel to give Himself so closely to a person and then be ignored while He remains with them. Music can be extremely helpful here. If it is going to assist your congregation in keeping a prayerful focus, instrumental music might be best. If it is not instrumental, at least it must be quiet. Even something as meditative as a Taizé theme (a continual melodic repetition of a brief scriptural theme) could be appropriate here.[75]

If the meditation does have extensive texts, the lyrics must not detract from the Eucharistic theme, though they may tie it, for instance, to themes of the day's readings, a feast, or the liturgical season. Still, the simpler, the better. Key and instrumental choice are not concerning here unless they can somehow constitute a distraction. A gentle melody, communicative of awe or peace, is ideal.[76]

Rhythm, however, must be handled carefully. It cannot be motivating or stirring to action; instead it must help to still listeners and direct them toward an inward focus. Rhythm is de-emphasized

---

[75] Such meditations include "Adoramus Te Christe," "Jesus Remember Me," "Nada te Turbe," "Ubi Caritas," and "Dona Nobis Pacem." Musical resources are available from the Taizé monastery at https://www.taize.fr/en_rubrique2603.html.

[76] Songs such as "What Wondrous Love Is This?," "Holy Is His Name," "Gentle Woman," or "The Prayer of Saint Francis" employ the musical principles sought for this moment.

here almost more than anywhere else in the Mass. The opposite will be true in the song to follow, so this contrast must be great enough for the congregation to feel.

Finally, this is not a time for congregational singing, as souls should be individually occupied in thanksgiving, having just received Jesus. That means that this can be an appropriate moment to feature the highest technical proficiencies of your choir, if they contribute to the beauty of the meditation. For instance, a professional member of your choir who is capable of, say, Schubert's or Gounod's "Ave Maria," or a solo violinist performing the same, or a small group capable of the plainchant setting, can very effectively move hearts at this point.

Reminders for the Meditation after Communion

- Music at this point must assist congregants in maintaining a loving, prayerful focus on Jesus following their reception of Communion.
- In the minutes after Communion, souls are closer to Jesus than any human person can be to another. What might one say to God at a moment like this? Certainly, the most tragic thing a person could do is to ignore Him.
- Gentle instrumental themes or repetitive melodic prayer can aid in sustaining meditation.
- This can be a moment to let various technical aptitudes of your choir shine, as congregational singing is unnecessary. Therefore, your complete focus can be on creating the most beautiful backdrop possible for personal prayer.
- As a "mountain guide," you must now help your congregation peacefully breathe in the lofty atmosphere of the high peak of intimacy with Christ at which they have arrived!

Concluding Rites

The purpose of the Mass, if we have truly participated in the three-fold ascent of its mystic journey and consciously sought to invite Jesus deeply into our souls as we receive Him in our bodies, is not simply for us to enjoy the experience, with our pious eyes rolled back into their sockets. The pure enjoyment of His company is for the next life. The reason we have the Mass in this life is so that union with Jesus can change us to the point that through us, He can change the world!

It's exciting! In one sense, the Mass and the spiritual life are all about your individual soul—that is, the friendship God wants with you is exclusively with you, like no other soul, and Jesus would endure and offer the entirety of His sacrifice for your soul alone. However, in another sense, it's not "all about you" at all. It's about the world!

If we see things that make us wonder, "Why does God allow this?" or "Why doesn't He do something about that?," the answer is easy. He's trying to! To whatever degree His kingdom has not yet fully come, it is we who are preventing it! This is the consequence of God's radical respect of our free will and the reason for His intense longing for our consent.

God wants to change the world through His people. However, this can happen only if they are so intimately united with Him that He might work through them. Would the selfishness and violence and hatred that makes us suffer exist if we all allowed ourselves to be changed into "other Christs" for the sake of our neighbors? Do we see even more how the role of the musician, assisting souls in recognizing and responding to the reality of the Mass, is critical in a further way to the fate of the world?

The Mystic Design of Music in the Mass

The Recessional Song

Whereas the entrance song helped your congregation move away from the world, the recessional song must help them move back into it, but as souls motivated to live out the change that has occurred in them. This is the place for songs with themes of action! This is music to lead the charge into a new battle — the one not just for our own transformation but for the good of souls in the world!

Rhythm here can be emphasized (but not disordered) in a way it was at no other point in the Mass. We should indeed feel animated! Your choices in appropriate instrumentation are quite unlimited and can be as full-sounding as possible. Except for certain solemn points in the liturgical year, the tune and mood can even be cheerful and catchy, so much so that your congregation will emerge whistling into the world.[77]

If you have withheld these musical attitudes throughout the Mass, now is the time to express them completely! In the music of the Mass, taking full advantage of your range of expression as an artist, you have now assisted the bodies, hearts, and minds of your congregation through a transformative journey and as complete an encounter with Jesus as their souls can experience in this world. There is hardly another thing a layperson could ever do in a lifetime that is more impactful.

---

[77] Selections such as "We Are the Light of the World," "Faith of Our Fathers," "We Walk by Faith," "Be Not Afraid," "Let There Be Peace on Earth," "City of God," "Sing a New Song," "Soon and Very Soon," "Christ Be Our Light," "They'll Know We Are Christians," and "Lift High the Cross" all immediately come to mind as fitting this criteria.

Reminders for the Recessional Song

- Whereas the entrance song sought to create a distinct "break" from the world, the recessional song seeks to return us to the world.
- The song can reconnect us with the themes of service, evangelization, social concern, and all aspects of the mission of the Church Militant.
- Musically, this means that rhythm can be livelier and more emphatic than at any other point in the Mass, allowing us to feel physically animated and motivated.
- No restrictions with regard to key, instrumentation, or other concerns apply within appropriate reason, and the melody, ideally, is one so memorable that it stays with us beyond the church doors.
- In this final song, your music ushers us through the completion of the mystical journey of the Mass—bringing Christ into the world with us because of intimacy we have found with Him!

Conclusion

My musical friend, I am brimming over with joy and hope because you have allowed me to share these thoughts with you. You have now, in your skillful hands, your beautiful voice, and your mystic heart, a capability that even the greatest powers of the world cannot wield and cannot defeat. Your music, by speaking to our humanity in a language deeper than words, can help save our world by drawing souls to Christ where He most longs to encounter them — in the Eucharist.

As I think of how to thank you for the good you can contribute to the fate of our troubled world and how to acknowledge the fullness of what your work can accomplish, I am continually drawn back to a simple statement from one of the great authors of the "mystic map," Saint John of the Cross. He says that what prepares the soul to be united with God is the desire for God. I am afraid that what the souls of our time lack most is that desire — perhaps because they don't even know and have never been made to feel that God Himself waits for them in the Mass.

This is why so much of my hope is in your music. Nothing can spark and fan the flames of desire — of longing and love, awe and reverence — quite like music can when it is skillfully directed to the task. This is especially true if you, mystic soul, sing from your heart, where you experience that flame yourself. I hope in this book you have found useful tools to express more clearly the love that is there and have found even more to love about God in the unfathomable beauty of the Mass.

While most kinds of change take time, in your music, you have a match that can be struck to ignite hearts today. This very day, at the very next Mass, you can welcome and console Jesus on the altar with new love and use your music to awaken newfound desire in others. Though I call on all my brother and sister artists of every discipline to help return loving reverence to the heart of the human encounter with God in the Mass, it is your work that can affect change right now.

You are the heroes we need in our time. With all my heart, I offer you my thanks. Please be assured of my constant, grateful prayers for your success, and may the angels assist you always!

About the Author

God has led AnnaMaria, or "CC" to her friends and students, along a wildly unlikely journey. After graduating from high school at age fourteen, she embarked on a prodigious path as a classical musician, making her Kennedy Center debut as a solo recitalist that same year. She completed her Ph.D. in theology (liturgical studies) at Notre Dame at the age of twenty-four.

She went on to a career as a classical guitarist and operatic contralto spanning the United States and Europe in venues including Lincoln Center and Carnegie Hall. For years, her music diverted awareness from her counterterrorism work in Iraq and Afghanistan. However, a leak of her investigative research uncovering the trafficking and exploitation of children outed her involvement.

This led to her public and governmental advocacy combating the issue. Reflecting on what she had witnessed, she felt God's call strongly in her life to offer more, and in 2017, she pronounced vows in an association of the faithful pursuing the canonical process of becoming a Society of Apostolic Life. (Learn more about the association's plans to serve God's most vulnerable children at www. stcatherinesmission.org.)

Now consecrating her life's work to the ends of her community, she has written on many topics, though none so important as the

Mass. Her music is scheduled for new releases on the Orpheus Classical label. A proud Navy veteran, she loves sailing, scotch, and cigars—which Mother Superior permits in appropriate moderation, but only if she shares!

Sophia Institute

Sophia Institute is a nonprofit institution that seeks to nurture the spiritual, moral, and cultural life of souls and to spread the Gospel of Christ in conformity with the authentic teachings of the Roman Catholic Church.

Sophia Institute Press fulfills this mission by offering translations, reprints, and new publications that afford readers a rich source of the enduring wisdom of mankind.

Sophia Institute also operates the popular online resource CatholicExchange.com. *Catholic Exchange* provides world news from a Catholic perspective as well as daily devotionals and articles that will help readers to grow in holiness and live a life consistent with the teachings of the Church.

In 2013, Sophia Institute launched Sophia Institute for Teachers to renew and rebuild Catholic culture through service to Catholic education. With the goal of nurturing the spiritual, moral, and cultural life of souls, and an abiding respect for the role and work of teachers, we strive to provide materials and programs that are at once enlightening to the mind and ennobling to the heart; faithful and complete, as well as useful and practical.

Sophia Institute gratefully recognizes the Solidarity Association for preserving and encouraging the growth of our apostolate over the course of many years. Without their generous and timely support, this book would not be in your hands.

www.SophiaInstitute.com
www.CatholicExchange.com
www.SophiaInstituteforTeachers.org

Sophia Institute Press® is a registered trademark of Sophia Institute.
Sophia Institute is a tax-exempt institution as defined by the
Internal Revenue Code, Section 501(c)(3). Tax ID 22-2548708.